What people are saying about …

Thriving in Babylon

"*Thriving in Babylon* is right on the money! While much of the church has been fumbling around trying to find the right biblical example, Larry Osborne cuts to the chase, showing us precisely how to let our witness cut through the culture for the greatest impact of the gospel."

Ray Bentley, senior pastor of Maranatha Chapel, San Diego, California

"A provocatively inspiring guide, this book provides a brilliant template, helping us answer the proverbial question of 'What would Jesus do?' I absolutely loved it. Simply brilliant!"

Bishop Dale Carnegie Bronner, author, founder, and lead pastor of Word of Faith Family Worship Cathedral, Atlanta, Georgia

"This book is for all of us who are serious about having significant influence in our modern-day Babylon. The fresh applications that Larry draws from the life of Daniel are as relevant as today's headlines, challenging us to reconsider some old worn-out tactics."

Chris Dolson, senior pastor of Blackhawk Church, Madison, Wisconsin

"*Thriving in Babylon* is an utterly refreshing take on the 'culture wars' much of American Christianity seems to be obsessing over. With biblical insight and practical wisdom, Larry Osborne reminds us of what it takes for a community to flourish in exile. I highly recommend this book."

Mike Erre, lead pastor of Fullerton Evangelical
Free Church, Fullerton, California

"Trust me; this book will bless you! While many lament how Western culture and the church's place within it have changed, Larry is a welcomed and much-needed voice. He offers a clarion call of hope. God doesn't just want us to survive. He wants us to thrive."

Daniel Fusco, lead pastor of Crossroads
Community Church, Vancouver, Washington

"How Larry writes with such brutal honesty and, at the same time, inspiring hope amazes me. These pages drip with keen analysis, practical insight, and gospel hope. A must-read for anyone who wants to understand the current state, and possible future, of the church."

J. D. Greear, PhD, author of *Gospel:
Recovering the Power that Made Christianity
Revolutionary* and *Jesus, Continued …*

"Thoughtful and inspiring, Larry Osborne provides a fresh perspective on how we can live with bold faith in a post-Christian culture."

John Lindell, pastor of James River
Church, Springfield, Missouri

"Larry has an extraordinary gift for relating Scripture to our everyday lives. We are indeed living in modern-day Babylon. Every Christ follower should read this!"

Shawn Lovejoy, pastor of Mountain
Lake Church, Cumming, Georgia

"It is obvious why God chose Larry Osborne to be such an effective pastor in the local church. He has the ability to take the complex and often misunderstood ideas and communicate them in a way that is practical and applicable in a crooked and depraved generation."

Joby Martin, pastor of The Church of
Eleven22, Jacksonville, Florida

"In reading *Thriving in Babylon* I was led to thank the Lord again for Larry Osborne. His wisdom in bringing God's Word to bear upon our world is immense. Reading this book will answer many of your questions about living for Christ today and set you on a path to greater joy and victory in your Christian faith."

Dr. James MacDonald, senior pastor of
Harvest Bible Chapel, Chicago, Illinois,
and Bible teacher on *Walk in the Word*

"Awhile back I listened to a message by Larry Osborne entitled, 'Thriving in Babylon.' Honestly, it was one of the best messages I have ever heard in my life. When I learned that he was putting the content of that particular message in a book, to say I was pumped would be an understatement. Larry takes us on a journey with Daniel and shows us how, against incredible odds and in overwhelming circumstances, he was able to thrive in a culture that was as pagan as any of us have ever seen."

Perry Noble, pastor of NewSpring
Church, South Carolina

"This book is incredible ... possibly the best book ever written outside of the Bible. Buy it by the caseload and hand it out like candy."

Carolyn Osborne, Larry's mom

"Christians have two big temptations. The first is to hide from the world and simply throw truth bombs at its evils. The second is to assimilate into the world and compromise truth. Larry shows us a third way of truth and humility."

Darrin Patrick, pastor of The Journey, St.
Louis, Missouri; vice president of Acts 29;
chaplain to the St. Louis Cardinals; and
author of *The Dude's Guide to Manhood*

"It's easy for believers to feel disoriented in a culture that appears to be rapidly trending away from core biblical truth. Our tendency is to run and hide or attack and fight. Neither response is very effective. In *Thriving in Babylon*, Larry Osborne shows us a better way. In his engaging style he looks into the Daniel story we all think we know and unearths the ancient principles that allowed Daniel to thrive in a cultural setting that was spiritually toxic. *Thriving in Babylon* is now on my must-read list for church planters and anyone else committed to incarnating the gospel among those who have yet to clearly hear and see it."

Steve Pike, pastor and church-planting advocate

"Larry Osborne has lit a lamp for those who find themselves surrounded by the darkness of a godless culture. Instead of bemoaning the lost virtues of times past, he shows us how to live victoriously by engaging a world desperately in need of light. Larry helps us to rediscover Daniel as a guide in a postmodern world that other Christians have given up on. It's time we storm the gates and turn the lights back on."

Dr. Stacy Spencer, pastor of New Direction
Christian Church, Memphis, Tennessee

"Christians are called to live in a world that is often hostile. Yet our calling is to have hope, live in humility, and exercise wisdom. Larry Osborne provides a timely encouragement. *Thriving in Babylon* is filled with insight and contemporary relevance that actually, on more than one occasion, made me stop and think."

Ed Stetzer, executive director of LifeWay
Research, author, www.edstetzer.com

"I keep waiting for Larry Osborne to write a stinker. This is not it. This is his best book yet! *Thriving in Babylon* is a brilliant and timely must-read."

Steve Stroope, author of *Tribal Church* and lead
pastor of Lake Pointe Church, Rockwall, Texas

"The world is changing. Fast. The differences between now and just fifteen years ago are astonishing. How can believers deal with so much change, especially when it seems like a lot of it isn't going our way? *Thriving in Babylon* is a guide for all of us struggling to answer that question."

Greg Surratt, founding pastor of
Seacoast Church, South Carolina

"One of the most challenging aspects of Christian discipleship is learning how to be faithful to the gospel of Christ in a secular society. Too often we run to the extremes of fundamentalism or syncretism. In *Thriving in Babylon,* Larry Osborne shows us how to remain impactful to the culture around us, while remaining faithful to the faith. I highly recommend this book to anyone seeking to disciple Christians in this important aspect of following Jesus."

Harvey Turner, lead pastor of preaching and
vision, Living Stones Church, Reno, Nevada

"We are not in Kansas anymore, Toto. And just in case you haven't noticed, Larry Osborne has. With his typical brilliant mix of wit and solid biblical wisdom, Larry rightly divides and walks through the book of Daniel so you can rightly walk through the divided world we live in today. Pick up this book. You will be encouraged and challenged."

Todd Wagner, pastor of Watermark
Community Church, Dallas, Texas

The darker it gets,
the brighter our tiny light shines.

THRIVING IN
BABYLON

THRIVING IN BABYLON

WHY HOPE, HUMILITY, AND WISDOM MATTER IN A GODLESS CULTURE

LARRY OSBORNE

DAVID **C** COOK™

transforming lives together

THRIVING IN BABYLON
Published by David C Cook
4050 Lee Vance Drive
Colorado Springs, CO 80918 U.S.A.

Integrity Music Limited, a Division of David C Cook
Brighton, East Sussex BN1 2RE, England

The graphic circle C logo is a registered trademark of David C Cook.

Unless otherwise noted, all Scripture quotations are taken from the Holy Bible,
New International Version®, NIV®. Copyright © 1973, 2011 by Biblica, Inc.™ Used
by permission of Zondervan. All rights reserved worldwide. www.zondervan.com.
Scripture quotations marked ESV are taken from The Holy Bible, English
Standard Version® (ESV®), copyright © 2001 by Crossway, a publishing
ministry of Good News Publishers. Used by permission. All rights reserved.

The author has added italics to Scripture quotations for emphasis.

Some names have been changed to protect individuals and their stories.

LCCN 2014948804
ISBN 978-1-4347-0421-4
eISBN 978-0-7814-1327-5

© 2015 Larry Osborne

The Team: Alex Field, Karen Lee-Thorp, Amy
Konyndyk, Tiffany Thomas, Karen Athen
Cover Design: Nick Lee
Cover Photo: Veer

Printed in the United States of America
First Edition 2015

9 10 11 12 13 14 15 16 17 18

041019

To William, Katie, and Emma.
You are growing up in Babylon.
May you embrace it with Daniel-like
hope, humility, and wisdom.
Jeremiah 29:7

Contents

SECTION FOUR
Humility: How Credibility Is Earned

SECTION FIVE
Wisdom: The Power of Perspective

ACKNOWLEDGMENTS

I want to express my deep gratitude to Alex Field, Ingrid Beck, and the entire team at David C Cook. Your belief in this message and your incredible patience and flexibility with the process was beyond encouraging.

To the elders, staff, and congregation of North Coast Church, thank you again for making pastoring such a joy and for unselfishly allowing me the freedom to also minister to the larger body of Christ. Chris, Charlie, and Paul, you make coming to work a highlight.

A special thanks to Erica Brandt and my incredible wife, Nancy. Your careful editing and candid feedback made the final product far better than the initial pages you received.

Finally, I'm forever grateful to my parents, Bill and Carolyn Osborne, for modeling much of what I have written about in this book. Far too many of my peers have significant father wounds and unresolved childhood issues that sabotage their attempts to walk in hope, humility, and wisdom. I am not unmindful of how much easier it's been for me to trust my heavenly Father, simply because I was blessed to be raised by an earthly father and mother who daily reflected his love, grace, and faithfulness.

Larry Osborne
Oceanside, CA

SECTION ONE

DANIEL'S STORY

CHAPTER ONE

A MAN NAMED DANIEL

Famous but Unknown

He's one of the most famous characters in the Old Testament.

Many of us think we know his story.

We think we know it well.

But few of us really do.

His name is Daniel.

For some of us his name brings to mind a fiery furnace and a scary night in a lions' den. For others it elicits images of detailed prophecy charts with a lot of small print, dotted lines, and cross-references. Yet neither Daniel's miracles nor his prophecies make up the main point of the book that bears his name. They're an important part. But focusing on them leaves us with a highly abridged version that omits the most important parts.

IT'S NOT AN ADVENTURE STORY

Growing up in a Christian home, I always thought the book of Daniel was an adventure story. I assumed the main point was that God would deliver me from danger and persecution if I had enough faith and did the right thing. The fire couldn't harm me and the lions wouldn't eat me.

But if that's Daniel's main point, he and God have some serious explaining to do. When it comes to fiery furnaces and hungry lions, Daniel and his friends aren't examples. They're exceptions.

No matter how godly we become, our odds of surviving the martyr's fire and the lions' appetites are rather bleak. As far as I know, Daniel and his friends are the only ones who ever walked out unscathed. Everyone else perished, dying a horrible and agonizing death.

That's why it's such a huge mistake to turn Daniel into an adventure story. It not only obscures the main point, but it also sends a blatantly false message: *If we do the right thing, God won't let anything bad happen to us. He'll rescue us from the furnace and the lions.*

Yet nothing could be further from the truth. God's best have often suffered the worst this world has to offer. Ever since the fall of Adam and Eve, evil and injustice have had a field day. Bad things happen to good and godly people all the time. As if to drive this point home, the first story in the Bible after the fall of Adam and Eve is the disturbing account of a wicked brother killing his godly sibling in a dispute over how to best worship God.[1]

---

1   Genesis 4

And that's on page four.

The rest of the Bible is filled with similar stories. Unfortunately, my Sunday school teachers forgot to include any of them in our curriculum. These sordid accounts never made it onto the flannelgraph or into craft time. Maybe my teachers thought we'd stop coming if we ever found out.

I love the way the writer of Hebrews deals with this issue. He doesn't sweep it under the rug or attempt to dance around it. He goes right at it. After reviewing a list of men and women who walked by faith and experienced great success and incredible victories, he switches gears to turn our attention to another group of heroes: those who endured torture, jeers, flogging, chains, and imprisonment; those who were stoned, dismembered, and died by the sword; those who lived in abject poverty; and those who were persecuted, mistreated, and forced to live on the run, finding their shelter in caves and holes in the ground.

These, he says, were also men and women of great faith. Yet God in his sovereign wisdom declined to rescue them from their earthly trials and persecutions. Not because they were spiritual losers but because God had another plan.[1]

He chose to be with them *in* their trials rather than delivering them *from* their trials. We shouldn't be surprised when the same thing happens to us.

Jesus said his followers would face injustice and persecution. He experienced them himself. The same goes for all the apostles. In fact, fiery trials were considered to be such a normal part of the

---

1   Hebrews 11:36–40

Christian experience that the apostle Peter wrote that we shouldn't be surprised when they come our way. They are neither strange nor unusual.[1]

Now this doesn't mean that God won't deliver us, or somehow can't. He will and he can. But more often than not, our *full* deliverance won't take place in this world. It will take place in the next world. And that's why turning Daniel's book into an adventure story about God's power to deliver us from fiery furnaces and hungry lions is such a big mistake.

IT'S NOT A PROPHECY MANUAL

Adventure is not the only thing Daniel is known for. He's also known for his prophecies.

I remember as a young Christian being presented with detailed charts purporting to show how Daniel accurately predicted the *exact* day of Jesus's triumphant entry into Jerusalem. Better yet, the charts claimed to reveal in equally fine detail the sequence of events that will precede his Second Coming.

Daniel had some bizarre visions and dreams. No doubt some were from spicy shish kebab. But many were from the Lord. And those that were from the Lord proved to be amazingly accurate in their predictions.

Those who take a deep dive into Daniel's visions and prophecies concerning the coming of the Messiah are often blown away by the detailed nature of their fulfillment. Many come away with a greatly

---

1   1 Peter 4:12–19

increased confidence in the authority and reliability of Scripture as a result.

That's obviously a good thing.

But those who attempt to take a similar deep dive into the prophecies that have yet to be fulfilled don't always come away with such positive results. That's because Daniel's visions and dreams regarding the Second Coming of Jesus are rather cryptic. They deal with the future, so no one knows exactly what they mean or when they will take place.

As a pastor, I'm regularly asked by folks in my congregation to explain how Daniel's visions and other biblical end-times prophecies fit together. They want me to tell them exactly what each symbol means and how everything will play out. They want names, places, and specific dates on the calendar.

Now I could guess. I could speculate. Many of my predecessors and peers have done so. But something gives me pause. No matter how confidently they have asserted their theories and ideas, they've all been wrong.

Dead wrong.

If you haven't noticed, there's not much of a market for old prophecy books.

That's because for two thousand years, brilliant and godly Bible scholars have carefully studied Scripture and come up with theories and predictions that made a ton of sense at the time but now seem laughable. Some go back centuries. Some can be traced back a millennium or more. Some are rather recent. But they all have one thing in common. With the passage of time, their carefully researched *facts* have turned out to be wild *speculation*.

That's why I stopped making end-time predictions. I've quit trying to explain what I don't understand. I know Jesus is coming back. Of that I am quite certain. But as to exactly when and how he will work out all the nitty-gritty details, I'm a bit foggy. So I've traded my spot on the Programming Committee for one on the Welcoming Committee. It's more in line with my pay grade.

But having said that, I want to be crystal clear. I am *not* saying we shouldn't study Daniel's prophetic passages or do our best to understand what they predict. The same goes for all the biblical passages that speak of the future. They are, after all, Scripture. As with all of God's words, they are worthy of serious study and deep reflection.

I'm simply saying that we need to be careful when we make prophetic predictions because whenever we turn the bulk of our attention to deciphering the *obscure*, we tend to miss the *obvious*.

GODLINESS IN A WORLD GONE HAYWIRE

When it comes to the book of Daniel, his incredible example of how to live and thrive in the most godless of environments is the main lesson we don't want to miss. It's a template that's particularly relevant today.

We live in a world gone haywire. Our moral fabric seems to be decaying at breakneck speed. Things that were once shamefully hidden are now publicly celebrated. The previously unimaginable has become commonplace. In a few short decades our culture's response to Bible-believing Christians has gone from grudging respect, to a patronizing pat on the head, to a marginalizing indifference, to outright hostility.

It's mind-boggling—and a bit scary.

Yet Daniel steps into our confusion and fear with a book that contains the life-changing rebukes, correction, and training in righteousness we so desperately need.[1] He offers us a model for not only surviving but actually thriving in the midst of a godless environment.

He found a way, in a culture far more wicked than anything we face, to glorify and serve God with such integrity and power that kings, peasants, and an entire nation turned to acknowledge the splendor of the living God.

Which raises the question: *How did he do it?*

HOPE, HUMILITY, AND WISDOM

Obviously God's sovereign hand was upon Daniel. He was also a man of great faith. But there was something else he brought to the table. He lived a life marked by three qualities that are in increasingly short supply today.

Simply put, he was a man of great *hope, humility,* and *wisdom*.

These were the traits that set him apart. They gave him courage, credibility, and perspective. God used them to grant Daniel favor in the eyes of his captors and to propel him to positions of great influence. Yet sadly, when his story is told, these three powerful traits and character qualities get little attention.

It's an oversight I hope to rectify.

In the following pages we'll address each of these in depth. I'll illustrate where *hope, humility,* and *wisdom* come from, how they're

---

1   2 Timothy 3:16–17

developed, and the radical impact they had upon Daniel's response to the wickedness surrounding him.

But I warn you. If you choose to follow Daniel's example, some may question your sanity, while others may question your commitment to Jesus. Daniel's counterintuitive responses to wicked leaders, evil coworkers, and a godless culture are seldom seen today. In many cases, his responses were the exact opposite of what we have come to expect from our spiritual leaders and committed Christians, which might explain why we've lost so much ground in the so-called culture wars.

But before we dig into Daniel's story and his template for thriving in the midst of a godless culture, let's step back and take a closer look at the magnitude of the mess he found himself in.

It was awful.

The poor guy was an innocent bystander, caught in the backwash of God's judgment upon the sins of Israel and Jerusalem. Yet none of the injustices that happened to him were an accident. They were all part of God's master plan for Daniel, for the nation of Israel, and for us today.

Let me show you what I mean.

CHAPTER TWO

CAUGHT IN THE BACKWASH

How Big Is Our God?

Recess was the highlight of my elementary school experience. The homework, study drills, and tests were simply the price I had to pay for a sweaty game of tag, dodgeball, or football.

One year we had a particularly big event on the schedule. It was the final game in a schoolwide baseball tournament. This wasn't a lunchtime or recess game. It was bigger than that. It was scheduled to take place during our normal class time. That alone made it a big deal. But better yet, the winning team would be crowned as the Grazide Elementary School World Champions.

I was the pitcher.

It was an epic opportunity.

At least I thought so at the time.

CAUGHT IN THE BACKWASH

On the day of the big game, our whole class was amped. Our teacher warned us that if we didn't settle down, we wouldn't be allowed to play. We shut up like church mice. No one wanted to risk it. We knew she meant it. We flipped the switch and immediately donned our best behavior.

Unfortunately, we had a couple of kids in the class whose best behavior wasn't very good. They were out of control, pretty much on a daily basis. So it was no surprise when Marvin let out a yelp and took a wild swing at Steven, who had apparently snuck up and given him a wet willy.

Our teacher lost it. Mrs. Eisman (I'll call her Mrs. Eisman because … well … her name was Mrs. Eisman) screamed at the whole class. She marched Marvin and Steven off to the princi-pal's office and came back to inform the rest of us that we would spend the remainder of the afternoon reading and diagramming sentences.

Our big game was off.

Permanently.

We forfeited.

I lost my chance to be a world champion.

It was a bad day for a bunch of good kids who got caught in the backwash of Marvin and Steven's depravity.

I'm over it now.

Mostly.

Still, I learned an important lesson that day: *Sometimes the innocent suffer with the guilty. They can get caught in the backwash.*

Obviously, our little baseball game was no big deal in the bigger scheme of life. But when someone else's foolish or evil behavior destroys our health, our marriage, our job, or our lifelong dream, that's a different matter. It's not so easy to move on or get over it. But that's what Daniel had to do. He was caught in the backwash of God's judgment upon sins that were not his own. He had no other choice.

DANIEL'S DILEMMA

God had repeatedly warned the leaders and people of Jerusalem to repent and return to him or suffer the consequences. Yet they turned a deaf ear. They continued to disobey with high-handed arrogance.

Finally, God had enough. He brought down the hammer. He handed Jerusalem over to the wicked Babylonians, who besieged the city, raided the temple, and carried off the best and the brightest of Jerusalem's young men, including Daniel and three of his good friends.

Now I want to be clear. God didn't lose it like Mrs. Eisman did.

God doesn't have a temper problem. His discipline and judgment are perfect in timing and scope. They are never unwarranted or out of line. When it comes to dealing with his children, even his harshest judgments are carried out with our best interests in mind, always with the purpose that we may share in his holiness.[1]

The citizens of Jerusalem got exactly what they deserved and what they needed in order to turn their hearts back to God. Unfortunately

---

1   Hebrews 12:9–11

for Daniel and his three friends, they got caught in the middle of it all. They were carted off to Babylon with other young nobles, forced to enter the service of a wicked and egomaniac king named Nebuchadnezzar.

Yet Daniel never complained, never whined, and never gave in to despair.

He understood an important principle. He knew that God was in control of who was in control, even when the wicked gained an upper hand. In fact, it's the first thing he points out when he begins to tell his story.

IT WAS THE LORD ...

Daniel starts his book by emphasizing that Babylon's victory over Jerusalem wasn't a tragic triumph of evil over good. It was the Lord's will. It was God's doing. Here's what he writes:

> Nebuchadnezzar king of Babylon came to Jerusalem and besieged it. *And the Lord delivered* Jehoiakim king of Judah into his hand, along with some of the articles from the temple of God. These he carried off to the temple of his god in Babylonia and put in the treasure house of his god.[1]

From Daniel's perspective, it was God who gave Babylon the victory. It was God who turned the holy things in the temple over

---

1   Daniel 1:1–2

to Nebuchadnezzar. It was God who allowed them to be placed in the treasure house of a pagan god. And it was God who allowed Nebuchadnezzar to get away with mocking the God of Israel as an inferior and defeated foe.

Don't miss this. From the first page to the last, Daniel clearly saw God's hand in *everything* that happened. It's the foundation upon which his hope, humility, and wisdom rested.

WHEN THE LORD IS BEHIND EVERYTHING, IT CHANGES EVERYTHING

Frankly, there is no way to make sense of Daniel's response to the wickedness that surrounded him without understanding his deep trust in the sovereignty of the Lord. God's control was the lens through which he viewed everything that happened to him and to his nation. And it's the first thing he wants us to know before he dives into the rest of his story.

I am not saying (and Daniel isn't implying) that God's ultimate control of people and nations turns us into mere puppets on a string. We aren't mindless droids carrying out bit parts in a preordained cosmic theater.

We have freedom—a lot of it.

We can choose to live within God's will or outside of his will. Our choices really matter. They determine outcomes. We alone are responsible for our actions. We can't blame them on God or on anyone else.[1]

---

1   James 1:13–15

God's sovereign control simply means that in the bigger scheme of things, there are no accidents. His plans will not be thwarted. He is never surprised or befuddled. At the end of the day, everything will be found to have worked together for the good of his people and the glory of his name. Even when the wicked seem to prevail, he is at work. His kingdom will come. His will will be done.

For Daniel, God's sovereign control over men and nations factored into every equation. No matter what happened, he never forgot that his God was far bigger than Babylon.

Which invites the question: *How big is our God?*

HOW BIG IS OUR GOD?

If we're honest, I think many of us would admit that we sometimes fear that our God might not be as big as our Babylon. Now we'd never say that out loud. But it's how we feel and respond, both emotionally and behaviorally.

That's what makes Daniel's story so important today.

If we want to make a dent in our modern-day Babylon, we need to take our cues from the man God used to influence the original Babylon. And it all starts with a grasp of something we can too easily forget when caught in the backwash: *God is in control of who is in control.*

He always has been and always will be.

CHAPTER THREE

SURROUNDED BY EVIL

How Bad Can It Get?

If you feel as if our culture is headed to hell in a handbasket, you're not alone.

Most people have felt that way throughout history. Almost every generation looks back and wonders what happened to the "good old days." It's human nature. The evils of the past tend to fade from memory, while the injustices and evils of the present stand out in bold relief.

Perhaps that's why Solomon wrote, "Do not say, 'Why were the old days better than these?' For it is not wise to ask such questions."[1]

THE GOOD OLD DAYS

I have a pastor friend who regularly bemoans the lack of moral fiber in our political leaders, the media, and youth. He sees it as something

---

1   Ecclesiastes 7:10

unique to our modern era. Yet when I read the cultural critiques of spiritual leaders long dead, I'm struck by the fact that they said much the same thing.

None of them waxed eloquent about living in a day of righteousness and purity. I'm pretty sure they'd be shocked to learn that their days of evil have now become our good old days.

Our tendency to look at the past through rose-colored glasses isn't just restricted to the long distant past. It also includes the fairly recent past. Consider how many Christians look back at the 1950s and the days of *Leave It to Beaver* as the golden era of family values and godly culture. While they were indeed good times if you were a white middle-class suburbanite, they were hardly the glory days of family values and godly culture if you were a black family living under the last vestiges of segregation and Jim Crow.

That's why I cringe when I hear aging baby boomers decry the moral and political chaos that has overtaken our country. No doubt things are a mess. But I wonder if these former hippies have forgotten or simply romanticized the decadent and violent days of their youth.

Political leaders and presidents were shot at or assassinated about as often as rap artists are today. An unpopular war cost fifty-eight thousand American lives. Those who bravely served our country returned home to be treated with unwarranted scorn. Promiscuous sex and hallucinatory drugs were celebrated as the path to enlightenment. Race riots set major cities aflame. Police were called pigs. And no one over the age of thirty was to be trusted. Worse, some people wore leisure suits—in public—and they were proud of it.

IT'S NEVER BEEN EASY

It's never been easy to live a godly life. The pressures and challenges we face today may be daunting, but they're nothing new. I hear it was rather tough in the first century. It's still incredibly dangerous in Iran, Saudi Arabia, China, and many other places.

Granted, those of us who take Scripture seriously are often written off as ignorant or narrow-minded bigots in America today. And it's becoming increasingly common to be discriminated against for simply articulating biblical values. But let's be real. We've got it easy compared to many who are attempting to live their lives for Jesus in other parts of the world. We have nothing to whine about.

It's not illegal to pray. We can own a Bible. We can utter Jesus's name without fear of being tossed into jail or killed. When we refuse to bow down to the idols of our culture we may lose our job. We may lose some friends. But we won't be thrown into a fiery furnace.

Again, that's why Daniel's story is so important. It not only gives us a template to live by, but it also gives us perspective. Because no matter how bad things get, Daniel had it far worse.

When it comes to evil, Babylon has no equal.

Let me show you what I mean.

AS EVIL AS EVIL GETS

The Bible says that immediately before Jesus's return, a mighty angel will come down from heaven crying out, "Fallen! Fallen is Babylon the Great!"[1]

---

1   Revelation 18:2

Now that's strange because historic Babylon has ceased to exist and according to biblical prophecy will never be rebuilt or inhabited again. So why harken back to a kingdom that's already long gone?

The answer is simple. Babylon is the personification of evil. Even at the end of human history, it will still represent to the angelic host the worst of the worst. Nothing will ever reach its depths of depravity. Not al Qaeda. Not Mexican drug lords. Not the Tower of Babel. Not Sodom. Not Gomorrah. Not even Nazi Germany.

So what made Babylon so bad?

How did it become the biblical metaphor for all that is wicked and evil?

A Godless King

To begin with, Babylon's king was a godless ruler named Nebuchadnezzar. He was an egomaniac, known to be hotheaded, murderous, vain, unreasonable, and incredibly cruel.[1]

After conquering Jerusalem, he took a number of holy items from God's temple and brought them back to Babylon in order to put them on display. He placed them in the temple of his demonic god, Marduk. It was his way of publicly mocking the God of Israel.[2]

Later he built a ninety-foot golden statue as a tribute to his personal power and fame. He demanded that everyone bow down and worship it. Those who refused were immediately put to death.[3]

---

1   Daniel 2:5–12; 3:1–6, 13–15; 4:27–32
2   Daniel 1:2
3   Daniel 3:1–15

Another time, following a disturbing dream, he ordered his wise men and enchanters to interpret the dream. But in line with his unreasonableness and cruelty, he refused to tell them what he had dreamed. He told them to figure it out on their own. And when they couldn't, he ordered his executioner to kill them all.

Fortunately, before they could be killed, God revealed to Daniel both the dream and the interpretation. But had he not, Nebuchadnezzar would have slain all of them (Daniel included) for their inability to answer the most unreasonable of requests.

A Godless Religious and Educational System

Babylon was also known for its demonic influences. The state-sponsored religion was satanic, and the core curriculum in the schools of higher learning included a large dose of astrology and the occult.

In order to prepare for service to the king, Daniel and his three friends were forced to complete a rigorous three-year study program. It consisted of learning the language and literature of the Chaldeans, which means that it was designed to certify them as enchanters and magicians, experts in the dark practices of the occult.

Now I live in California, often called the land of fruits and nuts. Our legislature has passed some bizarre laws. Our courts have made some strange decisions. Our schools have introduced some weird curricula.

But I guarantee you, on the worst day, in the worst class, with the worst teacher, my kids were never exposed to anything as godless and flat-out demonic as the standard curriculum in Daniel's classroom.

No way.

Never.

Not even close.

None of my kids had to get a degree in the occult in order to land a good job.

A Spiritually Hostile Environment

To make matters worse, Babylon was fiercely hostile to the spiritual values Daniel and his friends held dear.

One of the first things they had to endure was a name change.

Daniel means "God is my judge." His Babylonian captors immediately changed it to Belteshazzar, which means "Bel's prince." *Bel* was a title for their demonic god, Marduk. The Babylonians used it in much the same way that we use the title *Lord* to speak of our God. It would be like having your name changed from Christian to Satan's Prince.

The same thing happened to his three friends. Their names were changed in a blatant attempt to blot out any connection to their homeland and their God. It was Babylon's way of forcing their captives to adopt a new identity and a new god.[1]

Even the food they were served attacked their faith. As wise men and enchanters in training, Daniel and his buddies were supposed to be fed from the king's table. It was a diet rich in foods expressly forbidden in the Law of Moses.

It was all they had to eat. That put them in a tough spot. It's not as if they had any kosher vending machines, delis, or grocery stores to turn to. They could either break God's dietary laws or starve to death.

---

1   Daniel 1:6–7

Rather than railing at his captors, Daniel calmly came up with a creative solution. He sweet-talked their guard into a ten-day test diet of vegetables and water. Then God stepped in. At the end of ten days Daniel and his friends weren't just healthy; they appeared to be better nourished than everyone else. So their guard let them skip the king's table for the remainder of their training.

But don't let this one small victory fool you. The cultural and spiritual assault against Daniel's values and traditions and God's law was immense and pervasive. There was no escaping it. When it came to staying kosher, he won. But when it came to his name, the things he had to study, and the wicked king he had to serve, he lost.

But that's not even the worst of it.

Daniel also had to deal with something that none of my Sunday school teachers ever told me about.

Something Else My Sunday School Teachers Forgot to Tell Me

Daniel and his friends suffered the indignity of castration. They were turned into eunuchs. Now I admit that Daniel doesn't say so explicitly. But it's strongly implied, as a quick lesson in ancient history and Jewish culture will reveal.

In ancient cultures it was incredibly important for a man to have a family, especially sons. They provided him with status. They worked his land and tended his flocks. They also served as a financial safety net. Without social security, pensions, or IRA accounts, there was nothing else to depend on in your old age.

In addition, sons provided a Jewish man with a legacy and a continuing place in the annals of God's people. Without sons, his family's allotted portion of the Promised Land would be handed over to others. His name would fade from memory. It would be as if he never existed.

That's why the Old Testament places such an emphasis on ancestry and family lines. It really mattered who begat whom. Those who were without offspring were looked upon with pity. Some even considered them to be cursed by God.

Yet when it comes to Daniel and his friends, there is absolutely no mention of any spouse or family in the entire book or the rest of Scripture. In a Jewish context, such silence is deafening.

Add to that the fact that powerful kings of antiquity routinely took the best and the brightest from conquered lands and brought them home. The best women were enrolled into the king's harem. The best men were placed into his service as high-level stewards and slaves.

Daniel describes the kind of young men who were imported from Jerusalem to serve in Nebuchadnezzar's court: "young men without any physical defect, handsome, showing aptitude for every kind of learning, well informed, quick to understand, and qualified to serve in the king's palace."[1]

Now obviously these are not the kind of men a king would want hanging around his harem. So to eliminate any problems (and to remove any chance of a testosterone-driven rebellion), kings routinely had such men emasculated and turned into eunuchs. In fact, the man in charge of Daniel's training was himself a eunuch, the "chief of the eunuchs."[2]

---

1   Daniel 1:4
2   Daniel 1:3, 7, 9, 18 ESV

THE DEATH OF A DREAM

I don't know about you. But when I consider all that Daniel had to deal with, I don't have much to complain about. All my excuses about how hard it is to live for God these days sound pretty lame.

Daniel was a young man with a bright future. He seemed to have it all. He was noble, a member of the royal family. And not just any young noble, he was the cream of the crop—first pick on the playground, teacher's pet, the kind of young man everyone wanted to be.

Then one day it all ended. A godless army besieged his homeland. His king surrendered. He and his friends were summarily hauled off to a strange land, with a strange language, to study a demonic curriculum in order to enter the service of an evil king.

Add in his castration and you have a really horrible, rotten, no-good day.

His dream had suddenly turned into a nightmare.

But in the midst of his nightmare, God showed up. He gave Daniel a plan and path to follow. And by following it, Daniel thrived in the most unlikely of places.

But that raises another troubling question: *Why would God let the bad guys win in the first place? What's up with that?*

CHAPTER FOUR

TOUGH LOVE STARTS AT HOME

Why God Sometimes Lets the Bad Guys Win

It was the end of a long day. We were all tired and hungry. My wife, kids, and I settled into the restaurant booth and looked over the menu. We placed our order and soon began to eat.

Then it happened. The kids snapped.

One took a couple of french fries off his brother's plate. That merited a quick shove, which warranted a return push, a loud yelp, and flailing arms. In a matter of seconds, Coke was spilled everywhere. Then the third one started to cry.

As a dad, I knew what I had to do.

I jumped out of the booth and dragged them outside. I gave the boys a quick and controlled swat to the seat of learning and a stern lecture, and then I informed them that their behavior was unacceptable. They'd blown their opportunity to eat. There would be no more food tonight and maybe not in the morning either.

The fighting stopped.

We went back into the restaurant. I figured I'd done my dad duty.

That is until the cops arrived.

They pulled me aside, questioned me, and then placed me under arrest. I spent the night in jail. You see, the kids weren't mine. They were seated two booths over.

Apparently you're not allowed to discipline someone else's kids.

Now before you stop reading, wondering what kind of jerk I am, I need to let you know that this event never really happened. I can assure you if anything close to it had occurred, my wife would have killed me long before the police arrived.

But it illustrates an important point: *A father disciplines his own kids, not someone else's.*

It's the same in the spiritual realm.

God's discipline always begins with those he calls his own. It was true of Israel and it's true of Christians today.[1]

Yet for many of us that can be confusing. At times, those who mock him, deny him, or high-handedly sin seem to do so with impunity. We assume God's judgment should begin with those who do the greatest evil. But it doesn't. It never has. It begins with us. And that's been perplexing to God's people throughout the ages.

---

1   Hebrews 12:5–8; 1 Peter 4:17

HABAKKUK'S BIG QUESTION

Consider the prophet Habakkuk. When God told him that he was going to lift up the Babylonians and allow them to conquer Jerusalem, Habakkuk was shocked. How could that be? The Babylonians were known as a ruthless and impetuous people, a law to themselves, promoting their own honor and worshipping their own strength. They hardly seemed like the kind of nation that a holy and righteous God would grant success to.

So Habakkuk asked why.

> Your eyes are too pure to look on evil;
>> you cannot tolerate wrongdoing.
> Why then do you tolerate the treacherous?
>> Why are you silent while the wicked
>> swallow up those more righteous than themselves?[1]

His bewilderment wasn't over the fact that God was going to judge the sins of the Israelites. He knew they deserved it. In fact, his book begins with a complaint that God seemed to be tolerating the sins of his people.

What threw Habakkuk for a loop was God's plan to use the wicked to punish the chosen. He couldn't fathom why they would be allowed to defeat and swallow up those who were far less wicked than they were.

---

1   Habakkuk 1:13

In response to his question, God told him not to worry. The sins of the Babylonians would eventually be dealt with. But it would be later, after he was through using them for his own purposes.

In response, Habakkuk wrote one of the greatest expressions of faith in all of Scripture. He finally grasped what God was up to. He was using the wicked to discipline those who were his own in order to bring about godly sorrow and full repentance.

> I heard and my heart pounded,
>> my lips quivered at the sound;
> decay crept into my bones,
>> and my legs trembled.
> Yet I will wait patiently for the day of calamity
>> to come on the nation invading us.
> Though the fig tree does not bud
>> and there are no grapes on the vines,
> though the olive crop fails
>> and the fields produce no food,
> though there are no sheep in the pen
>> and no cattle in the stalls,
> yet I will rejoice in the LORD,
>> I will be joyful in God my Savior.
> The Sovereign LORD is my strength;
>> he makes my feet like the feet of a deer,
>> he enables me to tread on the heights.[1]

---

1   Habakkuk 3:16–19

CHAD'S BIG QUESTION

I remember receiving a note from a guy I'll call Chad. He was upset about our church and a bit frustrated with God. He wanted to know why we weren't more aggressively defending biblical values, especially on the political front. He also wondered why God seemed to be standing idly by while the people he saw as sinners prospered.

He was particularly upset by what he saw as the irreversible advance of the gay agenda. He blamed it on churches such as ours that weren't fighting hard enough to stand up for "biblical values." He was sure that our failure to speak up enough was the main reason God was letting the "bad guys" win.

His note ended something like this: *I have no idea why God allows the wicked to triumph over the godly. But I do know that the moral collapse of our country can be traced to the gutless failure of churches like ours to step up and defend marriage and the basics of biblical morality.*

Chad was new to our church. I had no idea who he was. So I asked around. I found out that he was a self-proclaimed longtime Christian who had recently moved into the area. He had attended our church regularly for a couple of months, signed up to join a small group, and put some money in the offering plate.

Oh, and one more thing. He was also living with his girlfriend. Apparently they'd been together for a couple of years.

Since Chad's big concern was the growing acceptance of gay marriage in our culture, I decided to send him some verses that spoke to the issue. I also suggested that he read each verse slowly and carefully. And just in case he was a bit dyslexic, I underlined a few key phrases—especially those that clearly condemned the sexual relationship he was having with his girlfriend.

Apparently Chad thought Jesus's statement about choosing a life of celibacy and becoming a eunuch for the sake of the kingdom applied to non-Christian gays, but it was too much to ask of heterosexual believers like him and his girlfriend.

Unfortunately, Chad misunderstood how God's judgment works. He thought it begins with non-Christians. He figured his self-proclaimed faith in Christ should give him a little extra leeway, a free pass for living like a Babylonian with his girlfriend as long as he had a fish on his truck and followed Jesus in most other areas of his life.

But that's not how it works. God's judgment always begins with his own. Which is why he raised up the Babylonians and allowed them to sack Jerusalem, and maybe why he's allowed the modern-day sacking of American Christianity.

By the way, I never heard from Chad again. I don't think he appreciated the mirror I sent him. He preferred binoculars.

HOW IT GOT THIS WAY

Let's be honest. Chad is not an exception.

Our churches have long been filled with people who claim to be Christ followers but who live like pagans. Our lives have not been all that different when it comes to things such as divorce, sexual purity, forgiving those who wrong us, loving our enemies, slander, gossip, and the harder things of discipleship.

Perhaps we're experiencing something similar to what the Israelites experienced when they cried out for an earthly king. They didn't mind having God around. But they wanted to be like all the other nations. They wanted a physical and earthly king instead of a spiritual and heavenly king. Eventually, they whined enough that God let them have the king they wanted. His name was Saul. He didn't work out too well.[1]

Like Chad, many Christians seem to think that our rapidly declining cultural influence (and the outright disdain with which some of us are now viewed) is due to our lack of commitment to the so-called culture wars. They believe the tide would have been stemmed if only we had been more savvy or had more intensity and stomach for the battle.

But I think not. I believe the primary reason for our long run of spiritual and cultural setbacks is something else. It's *sin in the camp*.

Just as Achan's high-handed sin led to Ai's shocking victory over Joshua and the Israelites, our pattern of pick-and-choose morality has led to a series of equally shocking losses for the church in America.[2]

God loves us too much to let us stray for long. He'll do whatever it takes to ensure that we bear the fruit of righteousness. If it means pruning, he'll prune. If it means using his enemies to teach us a lesson, he'll use his enemies. If it takes letting the "bad guys" win to bring us to our knees, he'll let the "bad guys" win.

Which is why I wonder if many of the things we are most prone to wring our hands over may be God's doing? Perhaps it's his way of

---

1   1 Samuel 8:1–22

2   Joshua 7

purifying his church, bringing us to our knees, turning our hearts back to him.

I don't know for sure. He hasn't told me. Only time will tell.

But ultimately, it doesn't matter.

If we're caught in the backwash of someone else's sin, experiencing God's correcting discipline, or simply suffering from the natural consequences of living in a fallen world, the proper response is still the same. We're called to live a life of *hope*, *humility*, and *wisdom*.

Now I admit, those are hardly our most natural responses when under attack. In most cases, we quickly go to fight or flight. But the good news is that God doesn't just tell us what to do and leave it at that. He provides us with everything we need. He prepares us for battle before he sends us into battle. He gives us the Holy Spirit. He provides us with motivation and power. And he gives us the wisdom of Scripture to provide us with the game plan and instructions we need.[1]

THE TRAINING WE'D ALL LIKE TO AVOID

Unfortunately, he also uses hardships and trials to prepare us for battle.

In the school of life, Trials, Hardship, and Suffering are three classes no one wants to take. Only a masochist signs up for them. They can be excruciating. But they're necessary. Consider the old axiom: No pain, no gain. It's not only true in the athletic realm; it's also true in the spiritual realm. There's no strength without suffering.

---

1   Philippians 2:13; 2 Timothy 3:16–17; Psalm 119:105

Frankly, trials, hardship, and suffering weren't always necessary. They weren't part of life's original curriculum. But a couple of students named Adam and Eve failed a major exam, and ever since then they've been part of the core curriculum we all have to take.

So before we go any further, let's step back and take a deep dive into the important role that hardships and trials play in preparing us for spiritual battle. As we'll see, they serve many purposes. God uses them to thin the herd, to separate the genuine from the counterfeit, to expose our hidden spiritual weaknesses, and to awaken our dormant strengths.

They are the foundation upon which hope, humility, and wisdom rise. And they provide the spiritual boot camp experiences that turn raw recruits into fully mature men and women of God.[1]

---

1   James 1:2–4; Romans 5:3–4

PREPARED FOR BATTLE

CHAPTER FIVE

WHY OUR FAITH NEEDS TO BE TESTED

The Problem with Counterfeits

Years ago I bought a heavy-duty, brand-name pruner at a street fair. It looked great. It felt sturdy. The ad copy on the box promised superb performance. The salesman told me he'd never had one returned.

I thought I'd gotten myself a great deal. But the third time I used it, the handle snapped off. What appeared to be a high-quality, heavy-duty pruner capable of easily slicing through thick branches was in reality a cleverly disguised knockoff, broken by branches the size of kindling.

Yet there was no way I could have known.

It came with a brand-name label.

It felt solid to the touch.

The vendor guaranteed it.

It easily cut through the first few branches and had me completely fooled. But the moment it was tested on a larger branch, the truth came out. Despite its convincing aura of quality, it was a counterfeit piece of junk.

COUNTERFEIT FAITH

The same thing happens in the spiritual realm. We don't always know what we have in our hands because counterfeit faith looks an awful lot like genuine faith. Both can wear the same label, live by the same moral code, and spout the same theology. At first glance, there's no obvious difference.

In Daniel's day, counterfeit faith was rampant. Many who were physical heirs of Abraham passed themselves off as spiritual heirs. They maintained that anyone who was circumcised, participated in the Mosaic sacrifices, and could trace their lineage back to Abraham and Sarah was automatically a rightful heir to all of God's promises.

But many of them were Jews in name only. Their hearts were far from God. Their circumcision was physical, not spiritual. They bore the label without the reality.[1]

Today, many claim to be Christ followers but are not. When asked, they check the Christian box. They live a generally moral life. They show up at church for Christmas Eve, Easter, weddings, and funerals.

But in reality, their faith is nothing more than a cultural accommodation. It's the path of least resistance. They trust in their own

---

1   Romans 2:29; Jeremiah 4:4

righteousness, assuming that God grades on a curve. They lean on their own understanding, happily following Jesus as a cosmic consultant and the Bible as a helpful guidebook as long as what it says makes sense and doesn't cost too much.

Like the rebellious Jews of Daniel's day, their faith is counterfeit. But it's hard to tell if something is counterfeit or the real deal without first putting it to the test. And that's why our faith has to be tested. There's no other way to know the difference between the genuine and the bogus.

THE PROBLEM WITH COUNTERFEITS

The problem with counterfeits (in both the physical and spiritual realm) is that they look and feel so much like the real thing. If they didn't, no one would be fooled—and no one would be hurt.

For instance, if I take a wad of Monopoly money into the grocery store and try to buy groceries with it, the cashier won't check to see if it's genuine. There's no need. It's an obvious fake. No one would call the police. I wouldn't be arrested for counterfeiting. People would just shake their heads and laugh.

But if I hand the same cashier a wad of twenties (real or fake), the response will be markedly different. He'll double-check to make sure they are genuine.

He'll hold them up to the light to confirm the watermark or he'll quickly draw a line on each one with an iodine pen. If the line turns a golden brown, he'll put the money in the cash register. If it turns dark blue, he'll know that it's a fake, printed on standard starch-based paper rather than the cloth-fiber used by the US Treasury.

Without putting the bills to a test, he'd have no idea what he has. Though the differences between the real and the phony may appear minor on the surface, when it's time to make a deposit at the bank, the difference is immense. One will help pay his salary. The other will be totally worthless.

FOOL'S GOLD

Counterfeit faith is especially deceptive. It's a lot like fool's gold. It not only fools others. It fools those who have it. They think they have something of great value, when in reality they have nothing of value.

Even worse, the consequences of depending on counterfeit faith are horrific. That's why it needs to be smoked out as soon as possible. The tests are not for God's benefit. He already knows what's real and what's not. They are for our sake. We need to know the truth. And if we're depending on something that's not dependable, we need to know before it's too late to do anything about it.

The only way for the genuineness of our faith to be affirmed, its weaknesses to be revealed, or its bankruptcy to be exposed is for it to be put through the tests of hardship and suffering. Yet most of us are shocked and dismayed when our faith is tested in that way, especially when it involves suffering at the hands of the wicked. We're sure that our faith already passes muster. We can't imagine why it would ever need to be tested in that way.

The same mind-set was prevalent in Daniel's day. The priests, prophets, and spiritual leaders were well aware that God had a long history of putting his people's faith to the test. They knew the stories of Abraham, Isaac, Joseph, and Moses and the seasons of discipline and testing they endured under the strong arm of the wicked.

But they were sure that they themselves were immune from such testing.

In fact, as Babylon rose to international prominence, false prophets told everyone not to worry. They claimed that God would protect them despite their halfhearted faith and high-handed disobedience. After all, as sketchy as their righteousness and obedience might be, they were a chosen people, sons and daughters of Abraham.

Unfortunately, God didn't get their memo. He chose to send the Babylonians to judge the people's sin, reveal the bankruptcy of their faith, and thin the herd, separating the faithful from the faithless.

God still does the same thing today. He uses hardships and trials to reveal the genuineness or the fraudulent nature of our faith. And just as a hot fire is necessary to burn off the dross that refines gold, so too our fiery trials are necessary to burn off the spiritual dross and refine that which is genuine.

There's no way around it.

I wish there were.

But there isn't.

It's the test God has chosen.[1]

---

1   1 Peter 1:4–7; Acts 14:21–22

PUSHED TO THE LIMIT

When I say that suffering is necessary, I'm not minimizing the fact that it can be awful and devastating. Those who minimize the pain and anguish of genuine suffering with happy talk, clichés, and platitudes have never really suffered—or honestly read the Bible.

We're supposed to weep with those who weep. We're not supposed to smother them with banal truisms, out-of-context Bible verses, shallow advice, and links to our favorite podcasts.[1]

The fact is, we live in a genuinely fallen world. Our enemy is vile. The battle is real, the casualties tragic. We aren't playing war games. We're involved in a life-and-death struggle.

Yet despite the fierceness of the battle, we still have reason for hope. Though we are sometimes pushed *to* the limit, we will never be pushed *over* the limit. That's a promise. It's straight from God.[2]

Consider the dreadful trials of Job.

Satan was certain Job would walk away from God once his earthly blessings were taken away. But God knew differently. To prove the point, he allowed Satan to take his best shot (within strictly defined limits).

But notice that the purpose of Job's trials was not to see how much it would take to break him. It was to confirm and display the depth of righteousness that God knew Job already had.[3]

---

1   Romans 12:15
2   1 Corinthians 10:13
3   Job 1–2

Now I must adm... my knees grow weak. I qua... enduring anything close to the trials he face... miserably.

But I need not worry.

I'm not Job.

The Lord will give me Larry's test, not Job's test.

If my test rivals Job's, it will only be because the strength of my faith rivals Job's.

And therein lies an important principle. Those who walk away from God in anger and disillusionment in the midst of their suffering never do so because their test was too hard. They do so because their faith was not genuine.

It's a lot like my broken pruner. Its handle didn't snap off because the branches were too big. It snapped off because the pruner wasn't what it was advertised to be.

DIRTY TRICKS

By the way, it's not our job to determine if the faith of others is genuine or fake. We're supposed to use our trials and our Bible as a mirror to see how we measure up, not as binoculars to check out how everyone else stacks up.

We're not supposed to take it upon ourselves to weed out the genuine from the counterfeit.

That's God's job.

Jesus made it clear that we are to leave the weeding to him. He told a parable about a farmer whose enemy came at night and cast darnel seeds (a ryegrass that looks a lot like wheat until the grain appears) among the wheat. When it became obvious what had happened, the owner's servants wanted to go into the field and pull out the darnel. But he told them not to, lest they pull up the good with the bad.

Historians tell us that in ancient Rome the practice of planting weeds in an enemy's field was such a problem that they had to pass a law against it.[1] As you can imagine, a large amount of darnel would create quite a mess for a farmer. He'd have no way of knowing that his crop was at risk until it was too late. And by then, there would be nothing he could do about it.

Jesus is warning us that Satan employs the same dirty trick in the kingdom of God. He sows weeds among God's wheat. There are men and women in our churches who are as bogus as darnel, planted there by the Enemy. But it's not our job to jump in and fix the problem. We're too likely to pull up some of the good with the bad. We're to leave it to God. He'll send out his angels at the harvest and they'll do the job.[2]

FAILURE IS NOT FINAL

None of this is meant to imply that genuine faith doesn't struggle, falter, or at times fall flat on its face. Abraham lied, Moses had a hot temper, David committed adultery, and Peter denied Jesus. These four make up a rather elite group. Any way you measure, they're at

1   Craig S. Keener, *The Gospel of Matthew: A Socio-Rhetorical Commentary* (Grand Rapids, MI: Eerdmans, 2009), 386–87.

2   Matthew 13:24–30, 36–43

the top of the spiritual food chain. Yet all of them failed miserably, in ways that call the genuineness of their faith into question.

But in each case their failure was followed by something important. They repented, got back up, and continued to move forward.

That's what differentiates genuine faith from counterfeit faith. Both fail at times. But when counterfeit faith fails it stays down for the count. It withers and dies under the pressure of Babylon-like temptation or hostility.

Genuine faith responds differently. It refuses to stay down. It struggles to get back onto its feet. Empowered by the Spirit of God it finds a way to keep moving forward. It might run like a Daniel or limp like a Jacob. It might sprint across the finish line or crawl across the finish line. But either way, it finishes. It doesn't quit.

Make no mistake. God's children mess up big-time and often. But there is one thing they don't do.

They don't quit.

They can't.

God lives in them.

And God *never* quits.

CHAPTER SIX

WHY GOOD INTENTIONS, MORALITY, AND FAST STARTS CAN'T BE TRUSTED

Counterfeit Faith's Most Convincing Traits

Some counterfeits are far more convincing than others.

Let's look again at our modern currency. Most fakes are easily spotted. The cloth-based paper the US Treasury uses is hard to come by. That means that most counterfeits are printed on starch-based paper, causing them to fail both the touch test and the iodine test. As a result, only about 1 percent of the bills in circulation are estimated to be phony.

But sometimes the counterfeiters get their hands on the same kind of paper that the government uses. When they do, their counterfeits are a lot harder to detect. They stay in circulation longer. But eventually they're found out because even the best counterfeiters can't reproduce *all* of the authenticating details found in genuine currency.

For instance, every five-dollar bill and higher has an embedded plastic strip that is sewn in. It's located in a different spot for each denomination so that smaller bills can't be bleached and then reprinted as larger bills. There's also a vertical band that shows up as a different color for each amount when viewed under black light, and there's color-shifting ink that appears to change color when tilted in different directions. Then there's the watermark. It can be seen when held up to a light. It bears the image of whoever's portrait is printed on that particular bill.

Now obviously it would take too long to check out all of these verifying marks at the cash register. We'd wait in line forever. So the better counterfeits last for a while. But sooner or later something seems out of place. Someone looks more closely and the counterfeit is exposed.

It's the same way in the spiritual realm. Some forms of counterfeit faith are easy to recognize. Some take awhile to come to light. The phony faith of self-proclaimed Christians who live like hell is easy to spot. They don't fool anybody but themselves. The same for those whose faith is merely a matter of convenience or cultural conformity—they bail out and walk away the moment it's no longer easy or convenient to follow Jesus.

But some forms of counterfeit faith are far more deceptive. They mimic enough traits found in the real deal that they fool many—both outside observers and those who trust in them.

In Daniel's day it was circumcision, the observance of Jewish religious rituals, and a direct tie to Abraham and Sarah that deceived many. They thought that was all they needed to be right with God. They figured circumcision and rituals were enough to balance out their lack of justice, mercy, and humility.[1]

In our day, it's no longer circumcision, religious rituals, or ancestry that deceives us into thinking we're right with God despite a pattern of high-handed disobedience. Today it's more likely to be good intentions, high moral standards, or a fast start that causes us to have spiritual confidence where none is warranted.

So let's take a careful look at each of these three deceptive traits in order to see why they can't make us right with God or prepare us to face the hostility of Babylon.

Good Intentions

It's easy to confuse good intentions with reality. We do it all the time. Think of your neighborhood gym. It makes most of its money on members who never show up. They want to show up. They plan to show up. They pay good money to show up. But they never do.

The same thing happens in the spiritual realm. There are a lot of people who want to follow Jesus but never get around to it. Some, like the rich young man mentioned in Mark, are keen on entering God's kingdom, but once they realize what life in the kingdom demands, they change their minds.[2] Others respond to the equivalent of a spiritual infomercial by eagerly signing up on the spot. But they, too, never take the next step. They have the best intentions but the worst follow-through.

---

1   Micah 6:8
2   Mark 10:17–27

Jesus pointed out the deceitfulness of good intentions in a parable about two brothers. Their father asked them to work in his vineyard. One said, "I will." The other said, "I will not."

Yet neither did what he said he would do. The brother with the good intentions never showed up. The brother with the bad attitude changed his mind and went to work. Jesus then asked the crowd, "Which of the two brothers did what his father wanted?" The answer was obvious.[1]

Yet despite what Jesus said, many of us still tend to equate good intentions with genuine faith. If you don't believe me, just listen to the things we say at funerals. It doesn't matter how godless someone's life may have been. If we can find the slightest evidence of a fleeting nod to God or a momentary, passing desire to follow Jesus, we'll highlight it and assure everyone that the deceased is now in a better place.

The absence of spiritual fruit doesn't seem to matter. Nor does the presence of truckloads of fleshly fruit. It's as if the fruit of the Spirit has been relegated to extra-credit status, an optional accessory for those who are really into Jesus. And in its place we've designated good, sincere intentions as the ultimate proof of spiritual birth.[2]

Now I want to be clear. I am not suggesting that our salvation is something we earn with good works and self-discipline. Our salvation and security are found in Jesus. We can't earn what comes by grace.

---

1   Matthew 21:28–32
2   Galatians 5:19–25

But I am suggesting that we take Jesus's words seriously. When he said, "A tree is recognized by its fruit,"[1] he meant it. If a tree bears oranges, it's an orange tree. If it bears lemons, it's a lemon tree. It doesn't matter what kind of label someone tacks on it. It doesn't matter what kind of tree the tree wants to be. It doesn't even matter if the fruit is of the highest quality or scrawny and malnourished. A tree is known by the fruit it bears. Only a fool would claim otherwise.

This is not to imply that good intentions are without merit. Good intentions are incredibly important. Without them, we would never take the first step. Genuine faith always starts with good intentions. So does repentance. So does every step of obedience. But when good intentions are *all* we have, we have nothing of value.

High Moral Standards

Morality is another common source of false confidence and spiritual deception.

The *absence* of biblical morality is proof positive that I don't know or follow Jesus.[2] But the *presence* of biblical morality doesn't necessarily validate that I have a genuine relationship with Jesus.

We often equate an ethical, moral lifestyle with genuine faith. But Christians aren't the only ones who live to a higher standard. So do many who adhere to the teachings of Judaism, Buddhism, Islam, and other non-Christian religions. So do many cultists.

High moral standards can be attributed to a lot of things besides Jesus. They can be traced to a good family background,

---

1   Matthew 12:33; Luke 6:44 says, "Each tree is recognized by its own fruit."
2   1 Corinthians 6:9–11; 1 John 2:3–5

religious upbringing, a strong desire to please, fear, or even a diabolical plan to deceive (the apostle Paul warns us that Satan masquerades as an angel of light and his servants come as messengers of righteousness[1]).

I think of Jason. He was a model child growing up. His parents were stalwart members of the church. He won awards for memorizing Scripture. He never got into the slightest bit of trouble. He helped old ladies cross the street and piled up citizenship awards.

But after he went away to college everything changed. He quickly kicked over the traces—all of them. The prodigy became a prodigal—the quintessential wild child flirting with danger until he finally fell into disaster.

We were all shocked.

We thought he was going to be a pastor.

We never imagined he'd be a prisoner.

But looking back, it's obvious that his childhood religious zeal and outward acts of righteousness were nothing more than a reflection of his desire to fit in and please those around him. They were the fruit of conformity, not the fruit of the Spirit. In the presence of his outspoken Christian parents, schoolteachers, and youth leaders, he was everything they wanted him to be. In the presence of his hell-raising friends, he was everything they wanted him to be.

The young man we thought was a budding spiritual giant was actually a chameleon. It took a significant change in environment to bring the truth to light. That's how counterfeits are. They're hard to detect. The best ones take awhile to be exposed.

---

1   2 Corinthians 11:14–15

A Fast Start

The third trait that easily deceives and leads to a false sense of spiritual confidence is a fast start with Jesus. Those who make an immediate and impressive spiritual turnaround are often put on a pedestal. If it's especially dramatic or bizarre, we put them on the speaking circuit.

Now, all things considered, I'd rather have a great start than a bad start.

But make no mistake, a great start is no guarantee of a happy ending. It may even be the precursor to a tragic ending.

Jesus illustrated the folly of putting too much stock in early returns when he told a parable about a farmer who cast his seed on four different types of soil.[1]

Some of his seeds landed along the path and were immediately eaten by the birds. Jesus said that the hardpan soil of the path represented those who didn't understand his message, and the birds represented the evil one snatching away the seeds of the gospel before they could germinate.

Some of his seeds landed in shallow soil. They quickly sprang up. But under the searing heat of the sun (which Jesus equated with hardships and spiritual persecution), they quickly wilted and died, doomed by their shallow roots.

Some of his seeds fell into thorny soil. These also quickly germinated. But it wasn't long until the weeds (which Jesus said represented the worries of this life and the deceitfulness of riches) choked out the new growth, killing it long before the harvest.

---

1   Matthew 13:1–23

Finally, some of the farmer's seeds fell onto good soil. They grew to maturity and produced a fine harvest.

Now none of those who originally heard Jesus's parable missed the point. They lived in an agrarian society. They understood farming. No farmer finds comfort in seeds that sprout quickly but never produce a harvest. No matter how impressive the initial growth might be, an unharvested crop is an unmitigated disaster.

Ironically, some modern-day Bible teachers and theologians (who apparently know nothing about farming) have tried to turn this into a parable about eternal security. They use it as a launching pad to argue whether or not a genuine Christian can become a non-Christian.

But such arguments have nothing to do with what Jesus was talking about. He wasn't telling a parable about good soil going bad. He was illustrating that different types of soil produce different types of results and that it's foolish to put too much trust in the early returns. The fact is, no farmer (whether Arminian or Calvinist) rejoices in seeds or soil that fail to produce a harvest.

In order to survive and thrive in our modern-day Babylon, we'll need more than good intentions, high moral standards, and a fast start. We'll need a genuine and life-changing relationship with Jesus, one that produces a harvest of righteousness.

Counterfeit faith won't cut it, no matter how impressive the counterfeit might be.

But even more important, counterfeit faith won't cut it when we stand before God at the judgment. Jesus himself said, "Not everyone who says to me, 'Lord, Lord,' will enter the kingdom of heaven, but only the one who does the will of my Father who is in heaven."[1]

And that's why the testing of our faith is so important.

As I said before, we need to know what we have before it's too late to do anything about it.

---

1   Matthew 7:21

CHAPTER SEVEN

BOOT CAMP

How Trials Prepare Us for Battle

I live near Camp Pendleton, the US Marine Corps base in San Diego County. Every marine shares one thing in common. They've all survived boot camp. It's the experience that turns a recruit into a marine.

Boot camp is no picnic. No one but a drill instructor calls it enjoyable. But it serves an incredibly important purpose. And contrary to what many think, it's not to flush out the weak. It actually weeds out relatively few—fewer than 10 percent wash out. The primary purpose of boot camp is to make marines, not to break them. It's to prepare them for what lies ahead.

High-level athletes go through something similar. It's called training camp. Serious competitors learn early on: no pain, no gain. If a workout doesn't leave them sore, it won't make them strong. If their practices are too easy, they'll be gassed in the fourth quarter. To become a champion, they have to be toughened up. They have to be stretched and strengthened beyond what comes naturally.

It's the same in the spiritual realm. If we are going to survive and thrive in a Babylon-like environment, we have to be toughened up. We need to be stretched and strengthened beyond what comes naturally. We need a spiritual boot camp. We need some trials and hardships.

WIMP CHRISTIANS?

Every now and then I run across a Christ follower who has never really suffered.

Some would call them fortunate.

I don't.

I call them unprepared.

Those of us who have never been hassled or marginalized for our faith are ill equipped to face genuine persecution. We have little chance of *thriving* in Babylon. We'll be lucky to *survive*.

I'm reminded of a church member who came to me, crushed after he'd been passed over for a major promotion at work that effectively put a lid on his career.

He was an outspoken Christian.

His immediate supervisor was an atheist.

He was sure that was the reason he didn't get promoted.

Through tears he told me he was angry and frustrated with God. He felt that the Lord had let him down. He wondered what good it had done him to follow Jesus for all these years.

I didn't know what to say. I thought the main reason we follow Jesus is because he's God and he forgives our sins. I didn't realize there was a career advancement component as part of the deal.

To make matters worse, he had a prickly personality. From what I'd seen, he didn't play well in the sandbox. I wasn't surprised to hear that he didn't get the promotion.

He also had a long history of pestering me with a never-ending stream of articles and podcasts he wanted me to read or listen to. Most of them lamented the moral or political landscape of our day. Many were inflammatory and short on truth. Some were downright slanderous. All were heavy on the catastrophe side of the scale.

He was convinced that we were in the last days. He was sure the Antichrist was just around the corner. And he was concerned that I wasn't adequately attuned to the economic, political, and cultural disasters that were taking place.

Now I have to admit that what I did next might not seem very pastoral.

I told him the truth.

I reminded him that he still had a job, a decent one at that. It put food on the table and a roof over his head. In some parts of the world, he wouldn't even be able to get a job as an outspoken Christian. In some places, his faith could cost him his life.

I suggested that his failure to be promoted might be a spiritual boot camp experience. Maybe it was God's way of showing him he was too soft, not yet ready for battle. After all, if a lost promotion could put his faith into the ditch, there was no way he was ready to handle the genuine persecution he was so sure was just around the corner.

He immediately fell on his knees and repented. He thanked me profusely for telling him the hard truth he needed to hear. He went home with a new perspective, praising God for the job he had and the many blessings he'd been taking for granted.

If you believe that, I have some money waiting for you in a Nigerian bank account.

The truth is, he didn't appreciate my perspective.

He told me I was a lousy counselor.

He was probably right. But I still think I'm a lot more empathetic than a drill instructor.

FIVE QUALITIES WE CAN'T SURVIVE WITHOUT

As our society and culture become increasingly hostile toward Christianity and Christian values, there are some spiritual qualities that become especially important. There are five in particular we can't survive without. They're important no matter what the situation. But in a Babylon-like environment, they become absolutely essential. So much so that God will send us through whatever spiritual boot camp it takes in order to build them into the fabric of our lives and character.

The five qualities are obedience, perspective, endurance, confidence, and courage. Here's a look at each one and why these qualities are so important to our spiritual survival in Babylon.

Obedience

Obedience is the essential trait of discipleship. It's always important. It's the one thing that proves we know and love Jesus, and it's the ultimate goal of the Great Commission.[1]

But it's especially important in the middle of a firefight. There's no time for hesitation or discussion when all hell breaks

---

1   Matthew 28:18–20; 1 John 2:3–5; John 14:15

loose. That's why obedience to the chain of command is one of the first things a new military recruit has to learn. Survival and victory depend on it.

It's no different in the spiritual realm. Under the onslaught of a spiritual attack, it's imperative that we obey without pause. When God says, "Jump!" the only appropriate question is "How high?" on the way up.

Now you'd think that kind of obedience would come naturally to us as Christians. After all, we claim that our Lord is King of kings and God of the universe. Our theology says he doesn't make mistakes—or suggestions. He gives commands.

But let's be honest. When things go south, our theology often goes out the window. When the path of obedience doesn't make sense, appears too costly, or doesn't seem to be working, we're quick to blaze our own trail.

It's easy to obey God when we agree with him. But that's not really obedience. We haven't learned obedience until we do what he says despite our doubts, confusion, or concern that his way won't work out.

That's the kind of obedience Solomon had in mind when he exhorted us, "Trust in the LORD with all your heart and lean not on your own understanding; in all your ways submit to him, and he will make your paths straight."[1]

And that kind of obedience doesn't come naturally.

It has to be learned. And it's only learned in the framework of hardship and suffering, the spiritual boot camp experiences where we

---

1   Proverbs 3:5–6

learn that the key to success is found in *trusting* God, even when we don't *agree* with what he's up to or wants us to do.

There's no way to avoid it. Even Jesus had to learn obedience this way. The writer of Hebrews tells us:

> During the days of Jesus' life on earth, he offered up prayers and petitions with fervent cries and tears to the one who could save him from death, and he was heard because of his reverent submission. Son though he was, *he learned obedience from what he suffered.*[1]

A lot of the things God wants us to do don't make sense in a spiritually hostile environment. They seem counterproductive. Consider some of his most basic and well-known commands: love your enemies, submit to authority, and forgive as we've been forgiven.

All of these things are easy to pontificate about when our Christian values dominate the culture. But they aren't so easy to defend when our enemies are powerful, those in authority oppose us, and the culture at large mocks the very things we hold most dear.

But we must.

These are the things he commands.

It's what learning to obey is all about.

---

1   Hebrews 5:7–8

Perspective

Perspective is the second quality we desperately need in a Babylon-like environment. Like obedience, it's only acquired through the things we suffer.

Without perspective, everything gets blown out of proportion. We catastrophize. The loss of privilege becomes harsh persecution. Opposition becomes hatred. And every legal or electoral setback becomes cause for anguish and despair. In short, we evaluate and extrapolate without putting God into the equation.

Unfortunately, those who most lack perspective seldom realize it.

Why does a two-year-old think waiting five minutes is an eternity?

Why does a trust-fund baby think flying coach is the end of the world?

Why does a Little League parent scream and yell at an umpire's bad call?

In each case, it's a lack of perspective.

The two-year-old doesn't understand time. The trust-fund baby doesn't know how the rest of the world lives. And the Little League parent has no idea how insignificant his son's game will be in a few years—or days—or hours.

But in each case they think they're acting rationally. That's why they respond as they do. It's also why it never works to lecture a two-year-old, a trust-fund baby, or a screaming Little League parent about perspective. They think you're the one who doesn't get it.

But once we truly have perspective, it changes everything. It allows us to see the bigger picture. Consider the amazing lens through which the apostle Paul evaluated the many persecutions he faced. It's mind-boggling.

Here was a man who endured repeated floggings, beatings, assassination attempts, imprisonments, shipwrecks, and a life lived on the run. Yet he came to the point that he viewed them as mere momentary troubles in light of the heavenly glories to come.[1]

So how did he get there?

He got there through the things he suffered. Each trial left him stronger, more certain than before that he could handle the enemy's best shot. He learned to rely on the strength and power that Jesus provided, and he learned that it was enough to allow him to cope with anything that came his way.[2]

By the end of his life there was nothing the enemy could throw at him that he wasn't prepared for. He'd already been there, done that. He had a promotional T-shirt to prove it. Not even martyrdom could faze him.

That's what the backside of hardship and suffering does. It teaches us perspective. It takes the fear out of the things that terrify others. It keeps us calm when everyone else is panicking.

Maybe that's why the marines I've known who enter the civilian workforce seldom complain about office politics, workplace inequities, or the things that send others for a loop. They have a different perspective than most of their coworkers. They've already been shot at. With bullets, not words. They know what real danger and hardship look like.

---

1   2 Corinthians 4:16–18; 11:23–29
2   Philippians 4:12–13

Endurance

Endurance is a third quality we'll sorely need in Babylon. And once again, it's only found in the boot camp experiences that stretch and push us beyond our comfort zone.

I was a basketball player in high school. At least I thought I was. Though we were a championship team, we didn't win many games by a large margin. Most of our games were close until the fourth quarter. Then we'd pull away, leaving our opponents in the dust.

Our secret?

Our practices were harder than our games. Much harder.

Our coach ran us to death. When we thought we were too exhausted to run another set of lines, he'd have us run two more. We all thought he was sadistic. There were many days when we wished we played for another coach. But the day we lifted up the championship trophy was not one of them.

We didn't win because we had more talent than other teams. We won because we had more endurance. When other teams were gassed, we still had plenty left in the tank.

Looking back, I guarantee you we wouldn't have complained nearly as much if we'd understood the rewards our increasing endurance would soon bring. We might have even thanked our coach instead of cursing him under our breath.

It's much the same in the spiritual realm.

Endurance reaps great rewards. But it's no fun getting there.

Perhaps that's why Paul and James both made a point to encourage us not to give up when stressed or pushed to our limits. They knew what happens to those who cut bait and run away. They also knew what happens to those who hang on and let endurance finish its work. They knew they end up handling the kinds of trials that break most others.[1]

Confidence and Courage

Endurance produces the mental toughness we've come to call confidence and courage, both of which are desperately needed to survive in Babylon.

Any time we overcome something we once feared or dreaded, we walk out with a new level of confidence and courage that comes from conquering something we once feared.

False confidence and bravado are more hot air than reality. They tend to melt away the moment the real enemy shows up.

But the genuine confidence and courage that come on the backside of endurance are different. They run quiet and deep. They don't melt away when the enemy shows up or wins a battle. They settle in for the long haul, confident that a setback or two is no big deal.

In the athletic world, there's a reason why a veteran team almost always outperforms an inexperienced team in a big game. It's the confidence and courage that comes from having been there before. Veterans know that a couple of bad calls, careless turnovers, or even a big deficit can be overcome. They don't panic. They stick to the game plan, even if it doesn't seem to be working right away. They know how to win. They have the scars and the trophies to prove it.

In contrast, inexperienced teams tend to wilt at the first sign of trouble. After a couple of miscues, a growing deficit, or a bad

---

1   Romans 5:3–5; James 1:2–4

break, panic sets in. Their cockiness and hubris disappear, quickly replaced by fear and insecurity. Players sulk, point fingers, or jettison the game plan. In some cases they even turn against each other.

Yet the crushing defeat of an inexperienced team need not be final. In some cases it lays the foundation for future victories. It all depends on how the players respond.

If they curse their luck or fail to take responsibility, they'll keep on losing.

But if they lick their wounds, take a long look in the mirror, and set out to acquire the things they lack, a crushing defeat can become a major step toward future championships. In fact, it's amazing how many champions failed miserably the first time they appeared on the big stage.

It's no different in the spiritual realm. Our failures don't have to define us. It all depends on how we respond. If we curse our luck, blame others, and fail to take responsibility, we'll continue to fail. But if we face the facts, accept responsibility, and humbly get back on the right path, our failures can lay the groundwork for future success.

Don't forget that the vast majority of biblical heroes failed spectacularly at one point or another, many of them more than once. What set them apart was their refusal to let these failures define them. Instead of becoming angry and disillusioned with God, they repented and turned to God. And once they did, he turned losers into champions.

That's exactly what God wants to do with us today. No matter what we've done or where we find ourselves—and no matter if our scars and failures have been self-inflicted or innocently obtained—he wants to turn us into trophy pieces, displaying the incredible depth and power of his immeasurable grace and mercy.

But in order to do so, he asks us to embrace the boot camp experiences he chooses to send our way. It's how he builds into us the courage and confidence we'll need in order to face and win the battle.

Granted, it's not a lot of fun. At times it's miserable. But it's the only way to get there. As the writer of Hebrews said:

> No discipline seems pleasant at the time, but painful. Later on, however, it produces a harvest of righteousness and peace for those who have been trained by it. Therefore, strengthen your feeble arms and weak knees.[1]

So hang in there. No matter what you're going through at the moment, God hasn't forgotten you. He has a master plan. He may well be preparing you for a place called Babylon. And if he is, it's not so that you can survive.

It's so you can thrive.

---

1   Hebrews 12:11–12

HOPE: WHERE COURAGE IS BIRTHED

CHAPTER EIGHT

HOPE

Beyond Wishful Thinking

Daniel's suffering prepared him for Babylon. But it was his hope, humility, and wisdom that enabled him to thrive in Babylon. They gave him courage, credibility, and perspective.

Take away these three powerful traits and he would have been just another victim. But with them he was not only able to thrive but also to wield incredible spiritual influence in the most unlikely of places and circumstances.

In the following pages we'll look at hope, humility, and wisdom in detail. We'll define them, see how they affected his response to the people and evil that surrounded him, and explore what we can do to increase their measure in our own lives and walk with God.

We'll start with *hope*. It was the unmistakable source of Daniel's incredible confidence and courage.

ONE WORD, TWO DICTIONARIES

Daniel was a man of hope. Unfortunately, whenever I talk about the importance of his hope, most people have no idea what I'm talking about. They immediately think of something that has nothing to do with the kind of hope that Daniel had.

It's not that they're stupid.

It's not that I can't communicate.

It's that we're using different dictionaries.

If you haven't noticed, the same word can mean different things to different people. When my parents said a musician was *bad*, they meant he was not very good. But when my friends tell me, "That dude is *bad*," they mean he's phenomenal.

When a high schooler tells his parents that *everyone* will be at the party, he means most of his friends will be there. But when his parents protest that there's no way *everyone* will be at the party, they mean the entire student body.

Same words. Different dictionaries.

Language changes over time. Always has. Always will. That's the main reason we periodically need new and updated translations of the Bible. The original biblical text never changes. But the words used to translate the original text into our native tongue morph over time. If we fail to keep up with their subtle shifts in meaning, we'll end up with a Bible that no longer says what it was intended to say.

For instance, the famous love chapter in 1 Corinthians 13 reads rather differently in the old King James translation. The entire passage sounds like an exhortation to help the poor. It stresses the importance of charity. An uninitiated modern-day reader picking up a King James Bible would have no idea that it's a chapter extolling the importance of loving others.

That's because the Shakespearean English of the 1600s (when the King James translation was originally published) used the word *charity* to speak of a sacrificial love that puts others first. The readers of that day knew exactly what the passage meant. But today, centuries later, *charity* has come to mean something much more narrow—helping those who are less fortunate by providing them with food, clothing, or the money they need.

And therein lies my problem with the word *hope*. It has come to mean something completely different than the kind of biblical hope Daniel had. Today, the word *hope* has primarily come to mean either wishful thinking ("I hope you have a great vacation") or the mental gymnastics of positive thinking and visualization ("Don't give up hope, you can beat this").

But Daniel's hope had nothing to do with wishful thinking or positive visualization.

He didn't *wish* that everything would turn out okay.

He didn't *visualize* everything working out okay.

He *knew* (as in knowing a mathematical fact) that everything would turn out okay. He knew that God was in ultimate control of who was in control, as well as everything that was happening to him. And if God was in control, there was no need to panic—even if he sometimes had no idea what God was up to.

BIBLICAL HOPE

In other words, Daniel had hope in the biblical sense of the word. He had a deep-seated confidence in God's character and sovereignty. He staked his life on it. It was the lens through which he evaluated circumstances, made decisions, and determined his actions.

This is the same kind of hope that the apostle Paul refers to when he calls the return of Jesus our "blessed hope." Paul doesn't mean that we hope Jesus returns in the same way a lottery ticket purchaser hopes he hits the jackpot. He means that we are so certain that Jesus will return that it's become the organizing principle of our lives, influencing our priorities, moral standards, and even our willingness to be persecuted for his name.[1]

The apostle Peter uses the word *hope* in much the same way. When he admonishes us to always be ready to give an answer to anyone who asks a reason for the hope we have, he's not suggesting we compile a list of reasons we're hopeful Jesus *might* be the Messiah. He's exhorting us to be ready to explain why we're *absolutely certain* he is the Messiah.[2]

IT'S A PROCESS

This kind of hope isn't acquired overnight. It's something we grow into the longer we walk with God. It doesn't come from study-ing the Bible, knowing theology, or having the mental acuity to

---

1   Titus 2:12–13
2   1 Peter 3:15

block out negative thoughts. It comes from obediently walking with God and experiencing firsthand his character, power, and faithfulness.

Hope starts with a simple step of faith. When we reach the point that we believe God exists and know he rewards those who diligently seek him, and then begin to act upon our convictions, God shows up.[1] When we step out and trust him enough to do what he says, he comes through. And each time he does, we walk away with a greater confidence in his power and faithfulness.

At first glance, it might appear that Daniel's confidence in God was rock solid from the beginning. The first few verses of his book start out with a powerful statement of God's sovereign control over the affairs of men and nations. His description of Nebuchadnezzar's siege is almost serene. There's not a trace of panic. No hand-wringing. No questioning of what God is up to, just a simple statement that God placed Jerusalem into the hands of Nebuchadnezzar.

> Nebuchadnezzar king of Babylon came to Jerusalem and besieged it. And the Lord delivered Jehoiakim king of Judah into his hand, along with some of the articles from the temple of God.[2]

But it's important to note that Daniel's book isn't a diary.

It's a book written near the end of his long life. The opening verses aren't excerpts from a contemporaneous journal. They

---

1   Hebrews 11:6
2   Daniel 1:1–2

describe his perspective many decades later, as he looks back at events through the crystal clear lens of twenty-twenty hindsight.

When the Babylonians first showed up to put a stranglehold on Jerusalem, Daniel was probably as freaked out and despondent as you and I would be if a foreign power conquered our town, ransacked it, and then put us in shackles to cart us off to learn a new language and serve an evil ruler.

It's highly unlikely that as a young teenager Daniel was able to see the hand of God anywhere near as clearly as he saw it in his latter years. But with each step of obedience, Daniel's confidence in God grew. By the time he was thrown into the lions' den he was an older man (he was not the strapping teenager most Sunday school curricula portray him to be), spiritually mature enough to realize that God had a plan. And though he didn't know if it was life or death, he knew that no matter what happened, God's will would be done and evil would lose.

IT ALL STARTS WITH WHAT WE KNOW

In Daniel's case, his journey to steadfast hope seems to have begun with a simple act of obedience—his decision to stick to a kosher diet no matter what the consequences. It led to his first experience of God's miraculous intervention.

Frankly, we have no idea how much of God's law Daniel knew. He was raised in a time of great spiritual darkness. The priests, prophets, and people were far from God. That's why the Lord turned them over to the Babylonians. It's likely that his knowledge of Scripture and Mosaic law was rather limited. Prophets and priests don't tend to teach the Scriptures they ignore.

Yet there was one part of the Old Testament law that was widely known even in the darkest seasons of Israel's rebellion. It was the Mosaic dietary laws. And since Daniel knew them, he determined to obey them, no matter what the cost.

Upon arriving in the city, Daniel and his three friends were chosen for a special three-year training program designed to prepare them for service in the king's court. That meant they would be well cared for. It also meant they would be served from the king's table, which was decidedly nonkosher.

Daniel and his friends decided not to eat the forbidden food. They weren't jerks about it. They didn't cop an attitude. They politely asked the chief eunuch for an alternative. When that proved fruitless, they asked their personal guard if he would be willing to test them for ten days with a diet of vegetables and water.

Ten days was no big deal. God had given Daniel and his friends favor in the eyes of their guard, so he agreed.

That's when God showed up. At the end of the ten days, Daniel and his friends looked healthier and better nourished than everyone else, so the guard continued to serve them an unauthorized diet of vegetables and water for the entire three years of their training.[1]

But God did more than just give them physical health. He also gave them wisdom and insight into the things they were being taught. So much so that at the end of their three years of training they graduated at the top of their class. No one else was close.

---

1   Daniel 1:8–16

Imagine what that must have done to build Daniel's confidence in God's power and faithfulness. It was a huge hope-building experience. One of many he would have during his lifetime. By the end of his life, there was nothing that could shake his deep-seated optimism and confidence. He knew firsthand that God was in control, no matter how things appeared.

It's exactly the same with us. When we obey the light we have, God shows up. And every time he does, our hope grows stronger. We begin to experience biblical hope—the deep-seated optimism and confidence that comes from knowing that God can be trusted even when we have no idea what he's up to.

The good news is that biblical hope is not the sole prerogative of hard-core, type A, front-of-the-line Christians. It's the birthright of everyone who knows and follows Jesus. All we have to do is step forward and claim it. And we claim it by simply obeying the light we have, taking small childlike steps of faith in obedience to what we already know.

We don't have to worry about what we don't know. Because when we obey the light we have, God will not only show up, but he'll also give us more light. It's what I call the *dimmer-switch principle*: when we obey the light we have, God gives us more; when we ignore the light we have, he gives us less.[1]

And with each step along the way, our hope and confidence grow. Every time he solves a problem, walks us through a valley, or stands with us in the midst of a valley, we grow a little bit more like Daniel.

---

1   Proverbs 4:18; Romans 1:18–32

CHAPTER NINE
WHY I'M AN OPTIMIST
Lessons from My DVR

I'm a USC football fan.

I had no choice.

It's a family thing.

My dad was a graduate of the University of Southern California and a big fan of the Trojans. He'd regale me with stories of players and teams from his youth. I grew up knowing the names and numbers of players who graced the gridiron long before my time. Once he started actually taking me to the games, I was hooked. The pageantry, passion, and tradition (not to mention a few national championships) locked me in.

As with any fan, I hate to see my team lose. But some losses are worse than others. In the world of USC football, there are two games that matter most: the crosstown rivalry with UCLA and the annual battle with Notre Dame. But without question, the bitterest pill to swallow is any loss to Notre Dame.

It's not that USC fans hate the Fighting Irish (at least most don't). In fact, it's not a particularly heated rivalry. There's a ton of mutual respect. They've been playing each other since 1926. As I write this, they've evenly split twenty-two national championships and fourteen Heisman Trophy winners. Five of the ten most-watched televised college football games have been battles between these two storied programs. Most pundits consider their annual matchup to be the greatest intersectional rivalry in college football. Nothing comes close. And it's precisely because of this rich history and tradition that it has become the one game a USC Trojan fan hates to lose most.

Many of the games are vividly stamped into my memory, especially those that ended with a thrilling last-second victory or crushing defeat. But one game stands above the rest. It was not only a great game, but it also taught me an incredibly important spiritual lesson.

The year was 2005. USC was riding a twenty-seven-game winning streak. The Trojans were ranked first in the national polls and favored to win another national championship. But the Fighting Irish stood in the way.

It was a Notre Dame home game, so the stadium was packed with Notre Dame fans cheering on their team at a fevered pitch. For most of the game, USC seemed unsettled and out of sorts. They turned the ball over and squandered numerous scoring opportunities. Even though they were supposedly the superior team, they didn't play like it.

Then with just over two minutes left in the game, Notre Dame marched down the field to score an apparent game-clinching touchdown. With a 31–28 lead and hardly any time on the clock, the Irish fans went nuts.

Trojan fans sank into a deep funk.

Yet I still held on to a sliver of hope. Die-hard fans always do. *Who knows*, I thought, *maybe we'll run the ensuing kickoff back for a touchdown. Maybe we'll have a miracle finish. It happens. Why not us—why not today?*

But no such luck. Instead of a miraculous kickoff return, USC ended up trapped deep in its own territory. Then things went from bad to worse. As Matt Leinart, the Trojan quarterback, faded back for a desperation pass, a Notre Dame lineman broke through to toss him for a ten-yard loss at the fifteen-yard line. That left USC facing a third and nineteen as the final seconds ticked off.

The Notre Dame crowd went crazy. The Irish players chest-bumped. Their goofy leprechaun mascot cartwheeled across the field.

I lost my sanctification.

To this day, I can't get that play out of my head. And I can't watch it without reaching for the remote. But it's not to change the channel. It's to hit pause and then play it back in slow motion.

I want to see where the blocking broke down. I want to understand why Leinart failed to find an open receiver. But most of all, I want to take in the unmitigated joy and passion of the Notre Dame players and fans as they celebrate.

I count the chest bumps. I count the leprechaun's cartwheels. And then I watch it again.

Not because I'm a masochist. Not because I'm a good loser. But because I know how the game ends. I know that two plays after being sacked, Leinart will throw a miraculous fourth-down sixty-one-yard pass to Dwayne Jarrett. I know that as time runs out he'll sneak across the goal line with a little help from Reggie Bush in what will go down in USC lore as the "Bush Push."

In other words, I know that the good guys win (at least my good guys). And that changes everything. The same plays that once caused me to yell at the TV, toss the remote, and utter Christian euphemisms no longer faze me. A Notre Dame touchdown in the waning moments is no big deal. A devastating ten-yard loss is not so devastating. They just make the miracle ending all the better.

And then it hit me. Don't we claim to know how the game of life ends? And if we do, shouldn't that affect the way we interpret and respond to the Enemy's short-term victories and temporary advances?

If our sins are forgiven and our destiny assured, if we are joint heirs with Jesus and certain he's coming back to set all wrongs right, then despair and panic over the latest court decision, or even the steady erosion of morality in our culture, hardly seem like appropriate responses.

WHERE'S THE JOY?

I remember walking into our church years ago after a particular election that did not go the way most people in my church wanted it to go. You could cut the angst with a knife. I was shocked at how deep and widespread the sense of defeat was.

Had I stood up and proclaimed, "All is lost. The Devil has won. God has met his match. You might as well go home and hide," I would have been run out of town as a heretic. Yet that's pretty much how everyone was acting and feeling.

And it wasn't a one-time deal. I'm convinced that any non-believer listening in on our hallway conversations and small group gatherings, or reading our emails, text messages, and social media posts would be surprised to find out how often those of us who claim to believe that Jesus is sovereign over the affairs of men and nations fail to act and talk like it.

This is not to say that our electoral, legal, cultural, and moral setbacks aren't puzzling and frustrating. They are. It's a sad day when those who live godless lifestyles are lifted up as role models, when orthodox Christian doctrines are mocked, or when biblical values are criminalized.

But it's not the end of the story. These are simply the Enemy's short-term and temporary victories on the way to his great and final defeat. Today's score isn't the final score. Nothing can separate us from the love of God and the glorious eternity he has laid out for us.[1]

And knowing that should change everything about how we interpret and respond to the things that happen around us—even when they are tough, evil, and hard to swallow.

Fear and pessimism make no sense when victory is guaranteed.

THE LENS OF FAITH

Obviously, Daniel wasn't pleased to see his homeland ransacked, the Babylonians victorious, or his life turned upside down. He had plenty to be legitimately distressed about. But he also had God's promises. And it's here that Daniel made an important choice.

---

1   Romans 8:31–39

He chose to interpret his circumstances through the lens of faith. He responded in light of God's promises rather than in light of Nebuchadnezzar's successes.

Daniel knew God had warned the nation of Israel that they would be handed over to foreign nations if they failed to obey his commands. So when Nebuchadnezzar sacked Jerusalem and took Daniel and his friends off to Babylon, he accepted it as God's will. That doesn't mean he found it pleasant or enjoyed it. I'm sure he had many a sleepless night and a deep sense of sadness over what had occurred.

But his trust in God's ultimate goodness and power was stronger and deeper than his sorrow or confusion. He might not have understood everything that was happening, but he responded as one who knew that God was in control of who was in control, even when God's choices proved to be puzzling and disturbing.[1]

Daniel also knew that God had promised to restore his people and judge their oppressors once their season of discipline was over. So with faith, he embraced Babylon's temporary success as God's will. And with faith, he confidently looked forward to a better day when God would restore his people to a place of great blessings.[2]

The lens of faith is the key to seeing clearly when all hell breaks loose. It's the only way to make sense out of the senseless. And it's the only way to respond properly when obedience no longer seems to be

---

1   Deuteronomy 28–30; Daniel 1:1–2; Romans 13:1
2   Daniel was a contemporary of Ezekiel and Jeremiah. Both foretold the future restoration of God's people. He was also the recipient of dreams and visions that foretold the destruction of God's enemies and the coming of God's kingdom. See Ezekiel 34:27–31; Jeremiah 25:8–12; 29:8–10; Daniel 2, 9.

working. It's the lens through which all the great heroes of the faith viewed their lives and contemporary challenges.

Consider Abraham. Imagine how confusing and difficult it must have been as he trudged up the mountain to offer his son Isaac as a sacrifice to God.

The entire incident is mind-boggling—and if we're honest, rather troubling. God had clearly commanded Abraham to do the unthinkable—the irrational—the indefensible. There was nothing ambiguous about it. The command was crystal clear. He was to take his son up the mountain and slay him on an altar of sacrifice to God.

Yet the Lord had also clearly promised he would bless Abraham with descendants too numerous to count. A great nation would one day trace their lineage through him.

Frankly there was no way for Abraham to reconcile God's promises with his current reality. On the surface, they were mutually exclusive. A dead teenager doesn't give birth to a great nation.

Yet Abraham chose to view and respond to his circumstances through the lens of faith. He continued on the path of obedience even though it seemed like a path of folly. He figured that reconciling irreconcilable commands and promises was God's problem, not his. So much so that he figured God would raise Isaac from the dead—and mind you, this was long before Lazarus, Jesus, or any other examples of God raising anyone from the dead.[1]

Today, we have the same choice to make. Though our options are nowhere near as gut-wrenching or perplexing as Abraham's, we still must choose if we are going to trust God or not. When his

---

1   Hebrews 11:17–19

commands make no sense or the path of obedience seems as if it will only make matters worse, we have a choice to make. *Are we going to interpret and respond to our current circumstances through the lens of faith or are we going to interpret our God through the lens of our current reality?*

Ultimately it's a matter of "Who are we going to believe?"

WHO ARE WE GOING TO BELIEVE?

Satan and his minions are boastful liars. They want us to believe that their current victories are proof of their eventual conquest.[1] But Jesus says they're full of bunk. He's promised that the gates of hell won't prevail and that he'll return one day to set up his kingdom and cast Satan and his cronies into an eternal lake of fire.

So who are we going to believe?

The Gates of Hell

Jesus's promise that he will build his church and the gates of hell will not be able to prevail is well known. Most Christians are familiar with it. Many can quote it if given a running start.[2]

Yet many of us misunderstand what his promise means and overlook the audacity of his claim, myself included.

I always imagined Jesus to be making a guarantee that no matter what the Enemy threw at us, he wouldn't be able to defeat us. I pictured a fierce opponent on the attack as we hunkered down,

---

1   John 8:44
2   Matthew 16:18

protected by Jesus. I envisioned surviving the onslaught in much the
same way that the survivors of a tornado climb out of their shelter
after the danger has passed. They are thrilled to be alive. But there's a
massive mess to clean up.

You see, I was unfamiliar with the purpose of ancient city gates.
They weren't an offensive weapon. They served a defensive purpose.
They kept the enemies out. No one picked up a city gate and went
on the attack.

The idea of Christians hunkered down while Satan batters us
with the gates of hell would have been ludicrous to the people of
Jesus's day. They knew what gates were for. They wouldn't have
thought for a moment that the gates of hell couldn't defeat us. They
would have understood that the gates of hell can't hold us back.

The difference is huge.

One leads to a cowering, defensive, hold-on-for-dear-life
approach to life and faith. The other leads to an optimistic, confident, give-me-your-best-shot approach to life and faith. One panics
and despairs when things go wrong. The other stands strong and
hopeful no matter what the current scoreboard says.

A Book Called Revelation

We also have a book called Revelation. Admittedly, much of it can be
hard to decipher. But one thing is crystal clear. In the end, we win.
Big-time.

As I mentioned earlier, I'm often asked by people in my congregation to preach on it. But most of them don't really want me to
teach through the book of Revelation. They want me to tell them
what the seven trumpets represent and if the moon will literally turn

blood red. And since I live on the coast, the surfers want to know if it's true that the new earth won't have an ocean. Because if it doesn't, they're not sure where they want to go.

In other words, everyone wants to know what all the cryptic details mean.

They're usually a bit disappointed when I tell them that the main purpose of Revelation isn't to satisfy our curiosity or give us detailed insider information about events far into the future. Those who are alive in the final days won't need a highly educated Bible scholar or prophecy manual to decipher all the cryptic and confusing symbols. They'll make perfect sense, just as the Old Testament messianic prophecies (which were equally cryptic and confusing) made perfect sense when Jesus showed up to fulfill them.[1]

In the meantime, there is one thing the book of Revelation makes clear. Jesus is coming back to set up his eternal kingdom. And when he does, he'll vindicate his followers and annihilate Satan and the enemies of righteousness.

Knowing that should change everything about the way we interpret and respond to our current realities, no matter how puzzling they may be. If we've read the book and believe Jesus, we know how the game ends.

And that's why I'm an optimist, no matter what the scoreboard says.

---

1   1 Peter 1:10–12

CHAPTER TEN

GIGO

How Input Determines Outlook

"How do you do it?" my friend asked.

"How do I do what?" I replied.

"How do you keep from being depressed all the time? You're well read. You know what's going on in the world. How do you keep from letting it drag you down?"

"It's simple," I told him. "I avoid the GIGO trap."

When he asked me what I meant, I explained that GIGO is an old axiom from the early days of computing. It stands for *garbage in, garbage out*. It's based on the simple fact that faulty data produces faulty results.

It's still true today. It doesn't matter how powerful our latest computers may be, if we feed them wrong numbers, they spit out wrong answers.

I told my friend that a large part of his depression was an input problem. He had become a magnet for bad news and distressing information. Every news cycle left him increasingly dejected by the political, economic, cultural, and spiritual trajectory of our country and world. It had finally reached a tipping point. He could hardly sleep at night.

So I gave him an assignment. I asked him to take a four-week break from *everything* he was currently reading, listening to, or watching that in any way analyzed the news, current events, or culture.

I asked him to go cold turkey.

No Christian or secular talk radio, no TV news analysts, no editorials, no partisan magazines, and no online blogs designed to inform him about the news behind the news.

He looked at me aghast. "How will I know what's going on?" he asked.

I told him he could still get the news, but he had to read it online and it had to be straight news, not analysis. (And yes, I know there is technically no such thing as straight news. Even the briefest synopsis is presented through the lens and bias of the reporter or editorial staff. But you get the idea.)

"It's just four weeks," I said. "Pretend you're on a long vacation."

He reluctantly agreed.

When I saw him a month later, I asked him how it was going.

"It's amazing," he said. "I'm sleeping better and I'm worrying less. I hope it's not just because I've got my head stuck in the sand."

I assured him that wasn't the case. His outlook and emotional state hadn't changed because he'd stuck his head in the sand. They had changed because he'd stopped wrapping his mind around every *crisis du jour.*

THE RATINGS GAME

My friend didn't realize that there will always be a crisis du jour. We live in a fallen world. Something is always going to be broken or breaking. But the normal crisis du jour becomes a CRISIS DU JOUR when it's amplified by something called the ratings game.

Let me explain.

Audience ratings are the lifeblood of the media, whether Christian or secular. Without listeners and readers there would be no advertising revenue, no product sales, and no donations. So it should come as no surprise that gaining and maintaining a significant market share is an underlying consideration in everything the media does.

As an author, I get it. I can't expect publishers to continue publishing my books if no one buys them. It's the same for every TV host, radio personality, magazine, or ministry. If they fail to maintain their listeners and readers, they won't be around for long.

Unfortunately, this creates enormous pressure to keep your audience fully engaged. Thus the constant emphasis on the latest crisis du jour. Panic and fear sell. They're riveting and keep listeners and readers coming back for more. They don't want to miss anything.

Frankly, the media and most ministry fund-raisers *need* a crisis to motivate people to watch, listen, and give. If they don't have one, they'll create one. And if all they have is a small one, they'll make it into a big one.

It's no wonder my friend felt trapped in a deep funk. The more he listened, the more things he had to worry about. I'd have a hard time sleeping too. That's how GIGO works.

Now I want to make it clear that I am not saying our society, culture, and body politic are not facing some incredibly significant issues. They are. We have plenty of things to be deeply concerned about. Ignorance isn't bliss. It's folly. And discounting problems doesn't make them go away.

But the fact is, those of us who regularly tune in to our favorite news analysis or talk radio host in order to "stay informed" tend to get especially riled up and depressed. Input determines output. When we're bombarded with a never-ending stream of crises du jour, each one presented as being massively important and bearing the potential to destroy everything we hold dear, it's no wonder we lose hope.

When we focus on the size of our problems, we forget the size of our God.

HOW BIG IS OUR GOD?

God has promised to work in *all* things together for the good of those who love him and are called according to his purpose. That's not to say everything that happens is good. It is to say nothing is beyond his ability to redeem or overcome for his good purposes.[1]

He took Damnable Friday and turned it into Good Friday. The crucifixion of Jesus was the greatest act of injustice and triumph of evil that will ever take place. Yet today we celebrate it because when Sunday came everything changed.

We have a God who allowed all but one of the apostles to be martyred. It must have looked like a devastating setback at the time.

---

1   Romans 8:28–39

Yet the blood of the martyrs turned into the seed of the church. And as always happens, Satan's seeming victory was nothing more than another step toward his ultimate defeat.

Nothing has changed. Our God is still at work even when it looks as if all is about to be lost. He's never surprised. He's never overmatched.

Consider how bleak things looked when China was overrun by atheistic communism. It looked as if the bad guys had won. Missionaries were kicked out. Christians were harshly persecuted. The gospel was forced underground and seemingly silenced. Western Christians wrung their hands, worried that the menacing red tide of communism would spread across the globe.

But what Mao Tse-tung and his allies meant for evil, God used for good. Eventually, the spiritual emptiness of atheistic communism was exposed. In the meantime, the gospel that had appeared to be silenced was in reality flourishing in a vibrant underground house church movement that far exceeded anything found in the good old days when China was open to Western missionaries.

It's still the same. The increasing moral and cultural decay of our society is not something God was unprepared for. It's not beyond his power to redeem. He has a plan. It's not going to be thwarted.

I may not always understand his plan or agree with his timing. But the last time I looked, he's God and I'm not. So I've chosen to make sure that God's character, power, and promises are always a major part of my input. I refuse to analyze the present and forecast the future without including them in the equation. Because to do so makes for some really bad math and some really goofy conclusions.[1]

---

1   1 John 5:3–4, 19; Psalm 23:4–5

ADVICE FROM PRISON

Apparently, the apostle Paul had a similar perspective. We get a glimpse into his thought process in a letter he wrote to the Christians in Philippi. Writing from a Roman prison (remember, there was no ACLU to make sure the food was tasty and the exercise yard well equipped), he shared with his readers the secret to his personal optimism and his ability to cope with anything thrown his way.

When anxious or worried about anything, he prayed about it. But along with his request for a change in circumstances, he made sure that he also included a recitation of the many things he had to be thankful for. He exhorted his readers to do the same, penning these words of advice.

> Finally, brothers and sisters, whatever is true, whatever is noble, whatever is right, whatever is pure, whatever is lovely, whatever is admirable—if anything is excellent or praiseworthy—think about such things. Whatever you have learned or received or heard from me, or seen in me—put it into practice. And the God of peace will be with you.[1]

In other words, Paul understood and applied the GIGO principle. He knew that the thoughts he put in determined the feelings that came out. Which is why—despite his many beatings, imprisonments, and a life spent on the run due to growing hostility toward

---

1   Philippians 4:8–9

his faith in Jesus—he was able to view them as mere momentary troubles in light of the blessings to come.[1]

If we want to experience Daniel-like courage and Paul-like peace, we need to follow their example. Instead of letting our friends, the media, and the latest crisis du jour determine our outlook, we'll need to let Scripture, our personal experiences of God's power, and his many promises determine our outlook.

For some of us that will mean hitting the mute button in order to silence the panicked voices that have been feeding our fear and drowning out our hope. Because, ultimately, it's not our circumstances that determine our outlook; it's the way we *interpret* our circumstances that determines our outlook.

That's how GIGO works.

That's how FAITH works.

---

1   2 Corinthians 4:16–18

CHAPTER ELEVEN

HOPE KILLERS

The Curse of Conspiracy Theories and Catastrophizing

In the early years of computing, both data storage and memory were expensive, so many programmers saved precious bytes by using only two digits to signify a calendar year.

It worked fine—for a while.

But decades later, as the new millennium approached, it suddenly dawned on some of them that these older computers and programs wouldn't be able to tell the difference between the year 1900 and the year 2000.

While many experts viewed this as no big deal, a number of others sounded the alarm. They were convinced that most older programs and hardware would need an accurate date in order to function properly. So they predicted a massive wave of breakdowns and failures when the clock struck midnight, January 1, 2000.

They called it the Y2K bug. They claimed it would produce the mother of all computer glitches. They warned of elevators suddenly stuck, cars stalling, airplanes crashing, and nuclear plants melting down. Many feared it would usher in a worldwide economic crisis.

Their concerns created quite a stir, especially among folks who were prone to buy into conspiracy theories and catastrophizing. By mid-1999 I was under immense pressure from a small but vocal contingent in my church to set up a co-op food bank, preach Y2K sermons, and prepare our congregation for the looming disaster.

When I resisted, they plied me with books and tapes. I remember one particularly harrowing recording in which an influential Christian voice at the time predicted the total breakdown of American society, massive civil disobedience, looting, food shortages, and a potential worldwide economic collapse followed by global conflict as dictators seized the opportunity.

A DEBATE I COULDN'T WIN

When I pushed back and pointed out that the internal clocks in the computers of that era were notoriously inaccurate—which should have already resulted in reports of numerous stuck elevators and immobilized automobiles—I was sloughed off. They had their own experts telling them differently.

When I pointed out that real-life computer programmers and the government didn't seem too concerned, they told me it was due to a conspiracy of silence. The government had no idea how to fix the problem, so in order to keep the uninformed masses from panicking, they were covering up the problems as they frantically searched for a solution.

Others told me that President Clinton and his cronies were keeping it out of the media because they planned to exploit the resulting chaos and crisis by imposing martial law and installing him as president for life.

It was a debate I couldn't win. They had an answer for everything. That's how it is with conspiracists and catastrophizers. There's no way to convince them until after the fact. Their experts will always trump yours. And the absence of any hard evidence will simply be chalked up as further proof that the conspiracy is widespread and powerful.

ONE HUNDRED FIFTY SLOT MACHINES

When the dawn of the millennium finally arrived, there were a lot of parties, a few computer glitches, and no global disaster. The next morning the BBC compiled a list of all the reported Y2K problems country by country. Here's what their reporters found:

> In North America, even before midnight passed, some difficulties arose. About 150 slot machines at race tracks in the US state of Delaware stopped working. But according to John Koskinen, who has been leading US efforts to tackle the Y2K bug, the machines have been fixed.[1]

---

1   "Minor Bug Problems Arise," *BBC News*, January 1, 2000, http://news.bbc.co.uk /2/hi/science/nature/586620.stm.

So let me get this straight.

The conspiracy theorists and catastrophizers in my congregation wanted me to preach a series of sermons and start a disaster preparedness food bank to protect us from the devastating effects of 150 broken slot machines in Delaware?

Life is too short and hell too hot to waste time on such nonsense. Yet try to tell that to a conspiracist or catastrophizer in the midst of their panic and you'll be written off as a naïve fool.

But here's the real kicker.

Nothing seems to faze these folks. Once their latest theory has been proven wrong, they just move on to the next one.

MOVING ON WITHOUT LOOKING BACK

Most of the same people who hammered me about Y2K are still at it. With Y2K in the rearview mirror, they turned their attention to everything from Mayan calendars to blood moons. And once those proved to be no big deal they moved on to financial conspiracies and more secret schemes to shut down the government and set up a dictatorship.

Like Harold Camping devotees, they keep hitting reset. They never seem to notice that all of the primary sources of their information have a long history of getting it wrong.

It's enough to make me long for the Old Testament days when a prophet who warned of things that never happened lost the right to be heard—and sometimes his life.[1]

---

1   Deuteronomy 18:20–22

Today, those who cry wolf simply lie low for a season and then pop back up with a new conspiracy or catastrophe on the horizon.

LOOKING STUPID AND FEELING WORSE

Unfortunately, our propensity to catastrophize and buy into conspiracy theories undercuts our testimony and credibility with non-Christians. When the danger passes without a ripple, they rightfully look at us as Chicken Little or the Boy Who Cried Wolf.

It's no wonder they've stopped listening.

It's one thing to look foolish because we believe in the message of the cross and the power of an empty tomb. That comes with the territory.[1] But it's another thing to look like a bunch of scaredy-cats, warning everyone about things that never happen and fearing things that don't exist, all the while claiming to be ambassadors for the King of kings.

FEEDING FEAR

But as bad as the impact of catastrophizing can be upon our witness, its impact upon our spiritual life is even worse. It kills our hope and feeds our fear. We may talk as if we trust Jesus, but if we live most of our lives in a state of fear and worry, it's an empty cliché.

When we fall prey to conspiracy theories and catastrophizing, we not only end up worrying about things that are highly unlikely to happen, but we also forget that even if they did happen, God would still be with us.

---

1   1 Corinthians 1:18–31

Most of us know Psalm 23. Many of us can quote it. God is with us in the valley.

Most of us also know that Jesus promised to never leave us.

And most of us know God has promised to never give us more than we can handle.[1]

But once we slide into the swamp of conspiracy and catastrophizing, we forget all that. We end up fixating on the things we fear rather than the God we follow.

In addition, we imagine facing the things we dread with the spiritual strength we currently have. We forget that even if everything we're worried about happens, we won't have to face it with the spiritual strength we currently have. We'll face it in the strength God provides the day it actually happens.

He has a just-in-time delivery system.

He's never a day late.

He's never a day early.

Which is why if everything we dread most were to actually happen, it wouldn't be nearly as bad as we imagine. God provides us with what we need when we need it. He gives dying grace to dying men. We can't store up his power and provision in a warehouse somewhere.

I wish we could.

I'd have boxes of wisdom, peace, and power squirreled away.

But that's not how it works.

We walk by faith.

God calls us to trust him to provide all that we need when we need it. My guess is that if Daniel and his friends had known all

---

1   Psalm 23; Matthew 28:20; 1 Corinthians 10:13

they would encounter, their hearts would have melted. It had to be nerve-racking enough just to watch the Babylonians advance on Jerusalem. But had they known the rest of the story—that the city and temple would be sacked, that they'd be taken captive, carried off to Babylon, castrated, forced to study the occult, given new names honoring demon gods, tossed into a fiery furnace, thrown to hungry lions, and forced to interpret a dream without being told what the dream was—they would have collapsed in terror.

I doubt they could have imagined there would be any way they could survive all of that. Yet God showed up in each situation in miraculous and unexpected ways. And at the end of the day, he made sure they not only survived but that they thrived.

It's still the same today. If we claim to be followers of Jesus, there's never a good reason for panic. God loves a mess.

After all, it takes a mess to have a miracle.

CHAPTER TWELVE

TWO MORE HOPE KILLERS

Myopia and Amnesia

Asaph was bummed out. And it wasn't just because his parents had given him a weird name. He was disillusioned by the success of the wicked. Everywhere he looked, they were prospering, while everything he touched seemed to be falling apart.

It made no sense.

If being on God's side meant always losing, why bother?

If the path of righteousness was a path of failure, why take it?

Things got so bad that he almost walked away. But then God showed up. He pointed out something Asaph had failed to see. And once he saw it, everything changed. His anguish suddenly turned into praise.

Years later, he wrote a psalm about it. God liked it so much that he said, "Print it!" Today we know it as Psalm 73.

ASAPH'S MYOPIA

Asaph suffered from spiritual myopia. He could clearly see what was happening right in front of him. But he couldn't see what God was doing off in the distance.

As a Levite and choir director during the reigns of David and Solomon, Asaph experienced some incredible highs and devastating lows. He saw it all.[1] When he wrote Psalm 73 he was reflecting upon a particularly dark season when nothing was going right and the bad guys seemed to be winning.

From his perspective, the wicked were sinning with impunity. They had no conscience, no struggles, and faced no consequences for their actions. All the while, he couldn't buy a break. Despite keeping a pure heart and clean hands, his life was marked by constant affliction and struggle.

As you can imagine, it wore on him. He eventually became confused and embittered. He began to envy the success and prosperity of the arrogant. He questioned the value of following God.

Then something happened. God showed him far into the future. Asaph went into the sanctuary and for the first time saw with clarity the destiny of the wicked. It didn't matter how arrogant and successful they might appear to be. They were destined to be destroyed, ruined in the blink of an eye, swept away by terrors.

Suddenly, Asaph changed his tune. Maybe things weren't so bad after all. The wicked were still boastful, crowing with success

---

1   1 Chronicles 15:17. Asaph was the author of twelve psalms (50 and 73–83).

and mocking God with seeming impunity. But now he realized it wouldn't be forever.

Asaph suffered from a common spiritual malady. His real-life beliefs didn't match his theology. He understood God's goodness and justice theologically. That's why he started out his psalm (73) with these words: "Surely God is good to Israel, to those who are pure in heart." But by his own admission, he no longer believed it in his heart. His spiritual myopia obscured everything except his immediate circumstances.

That's why he went on to say, "But as for me, my feet had almost slipped; I had nearly lost my foothold. For I envied the arrogant when I saw the prosperity of the wicked."

The same thing happens to us when we get a bad case of spiritual myopia. We lose perspective. We judge God's goodness and power by our current reality. When things go great we praise him. When things go poorly we doubt him.

Spiritual myopia is a dangerous spiritual disorder. It causes us to call into question God's goodness and power. It kills off our hope, confidence, and courage. It produces boatloads of fear, doubt, and despair.

SEEING CLEARLY

The cure for physical myopia is found in corrective lenses. The cure for spiritual myopia is found in the cross and the empty tomb.

Through the lens of the cross we see the full measure of God's great love for us. He died for us while we were his enemies, steeped in our own sin and rebellion. He didn't wait for us to make the first move. He didn't foresee some great potential and decide, "This one is worth dying for."

No, it was all grace. It was completely unmerited love. And once that comes into focus, we no longer question his love or goodness. We may question his timing. We may question his methods, but never his love and commitment to our best interests.

Whereas the lens of the cross brings his love and goodness into focus, it's the lens of the empty tomb that brings his power into sharp relief. Once we fully grasp the implications of Jesus's absolute victory over death, we no longer question his ability to bring good out of the worst of circumstances and justice out of the greatest of injustices.

Perhaps that's why the apostle Paul prayed that those of us who follow Jesus would clearly grasp the full implications of the cross and the resurrection. He knew if we saw our life circumstances through the lens of Calvary and the empty tomb, we'd live with renewed confidence and courage.[1]

Frankly, when it comes to overcoming spiritual myopia we have an advantage over both Asaph and Daniel. Neither of them had a cross or empty tomb to look back upon. Better yet, we have the Holy Spirit within, testifying to God's love and power.

SPIRITUAL AMNESIA

The flipside of spiritual myopia is spiritual amnesia. Whereas myopia fixates on the present, amnesia forgets the past.

The children of Israel suffered from spiritual amnesia big-time. One of their most famous episodes occurred within weeks of being miraculously delivered from centuries of slavery in Egypt.

---

1   Ephesians 1:15–23; 3:14–21

As they headed off toward their new Promised Land, God instructed them to take a turn and set up camp on the banks of the Red Sea. The place he picked hemmed them in on three sides with water in front of them and mountains to the left and right.

Then God stirred the heart of Pharaoh to set out with his army to recapture the slaves he'd just let go. Trapped against the water and the mountains, the Israelites appeared to be easy prey. When they realized what was happening, they panicked. They cried out to the Lord in despair and accused Moses of bringing them out to the desert to die.[1]

It never dawned on them that God might be setting up another great miracle or a final judgment upon Pharaoh and his army. They were so dialed in on what God was not doing at the moment that they forgot everything he'd done in the past. It was as if the hard drive of their memories had been wiped clean.

Now it's easy to rip on their lack of faith and mock their forgetfulness. It's hard to believe they could panic so quickly after being delivered so powerfully.

But if we're honest, we're prone to do the same thing.

REMEMBERING CLEARLY

Fortunately, there's a way to lessen the impact of spiritual amnesia. It's found in practicing the discipline of gratitude, the habit of regularly giving thanks for all God has done.

---

1   Exodus 14:1–31

It's such a powerful preventive that God actually commands us to give thanks in every circumstance.[1] It's not that God needs the praise. It's that we need the reminder. A pattern of thanksgiving in every situation ensures we'll be able to remember in the dark those things we once saw in the light.

Practicing the discipline of gratitude doesn't mean we're supposed to artificially find the good in everything. Some things are bad. Some things are evil. Only a fool calls evil good. But in every situation, no matter how bad or evil it might be, there are things in the past and in the future to give thanks for. And it's in remembering these blessings that we find the courage to endure our present hardships and the evils we face.

CHOOSING COURAGE

Unfortunately, when it comes to spiritual myopia and amnesia we can go a long time without realizing that we have a problem. It reminds me of a friend who didn't realize he was terribly nearsighted until he failed a driver's license test. He thought everyone had a hard time seeing in the distance. The same with another friend's mom who thought her memory was just fine, despite the fact that everyone else knew she was losing it fast.

I know some folks who think their fear and angst are appropriate in light of their circumstances. But they're wrong. The moment

---

1   1 Thessalonians 5:18

our problems seem bigger than our God we are either seeing poorly or remembering inaccurately.[1]

And at that point we have a choice to make.

We can focus on what's going wrong or we can fix our thoughts on the cross, the empty tomb, and the plethora of blessings we have to be thankful for. If we do, we'll end up like Asaph and Daniel—filled with the hope, confidence, and optimism that come from knowing who's in charge and how everything will end up.

Or we can choose to fixate on the personal and cultural problems that plague us. If we do, we'll end up like the children of Israel—frustrated, angry, and panicked even when God is about to provide us with a great deliverance.

---

1   2 Timothy 1:7 ESV

CHAPTER THIRTEEN
FALSE HOPE
The Problem with Politics and Bandwagons

I used to lead a Bible study for a group I called up-and-outers. It consisted of baby Christians and some who had not yet taken the plunge. Everyone appeared to be highly successful, yet they had all climbed a ladder that was leaning on the wrong wall.

They knew it.

That's why they came.

By the end of our time together, they'd all come to know Jesus. It was a rewarding experience to help them scamper down the wrong ladder and start up the only one that could offer the spiritual and life fulfillment they were looking for.

In some ways, that Bible study group reminds me of many Christians I know. But instead of climbing a success ladder leaning on the wrong wall, they climb aboard bandwagons heading in the wrong direction.

Two of these bandwagons are particularly enticing. They each promise to halt the spread of evil and to ignite widespread revival if enough people jump aboard. One is labeled politics. It promises to halt the spread of evil and ignite spiritual revival through legislation. The other is what I call ministry on steroids. It promises to change the world by mobilizing everyone in support of the latest high-visibility, big-budget program or parachurch vision and ministry.

Unfortunately, both promise more than they can deliver. Those who promote them mean well. Those who scamper aboard want to make a difference. But in the long run, politics and big-budget ideas can't produce revival. And those who put their trust in them are destined to be disillusioned.

NO SUBSTITUTES PLEASE

Satan wants to destroy our hope. He knows that when we have Daniel-like confidence and courage, we won't be afraid to storm the gates of hell. So he'll do whatever it takes to kill them off.

But if that doesn't work, he has a plan B. He'll try to get us to place our hope and confidence in anything or anyone other than Jesus.

He convinced the Israelites to trust in horses and chariots, circumcision, religious rituals, and a physical lineage they could trace back to Abraham. He convinced the Pharisees and religious leaders of Jesus's day to place their hope in rigid spiritual disciplines and a bunch of extra-credit rules they created. And he convinced the first-century church in Ephesus to place their hope and confidence in good deeds, solid doctrine, and determination. He had them convinced that these were enough to compensate for their lack of love.[1]

He's still at it. Today, he's convinced many of us to replace our passionate hope in Jesus with a passionate hope in politics or the latest ministry on steroids. It's taken our eyes off Jesus and put our hope in that which can't deliver.

Let me show you what I mean.

TRUSTING IN POLITICS

There was a time not long ago when Christian leaders could swing an election. As a result, many pastors and leaders jumped on the political bandwagon. They saw it as the best way to shape society and save America. In some circles, an invitation to the mayor's office, the governor's mansion, or the White House became the ultimate sign of spiritual significance and impact.

The election cycle dictated preaching schedules. And those who failed to line up were widely criticized as being fearful or out of touch with the sins that ailed America.

Those who stayed focused on local church ministry and discipling were dubbed as old-fashioned and ineffective—fiddling while Rome burned. The slow and arduous task of introducing nonbelievers to Jesus and then growing them to maturity seemed antiquated when an entire city, state, or nation could be influenced by elections and legislation.

---

1   Revelation 2:1–7

Indeed, it seemed to work for a while. Elections were won and laws were passed. George Gallup Jr. dubbed 1976 as the Year of the Evangelical. *Time* magazine dutifully reported it as so.[1] Christian leaders such as Jerry Falwell, Pat Robertson, James Dobson, and others graced the covers of national magazines.

Yet despite all of these impressive political victories, the moral fiber of our country continued to deteriorate. Eventually, the electoral tide changed as it always does. And when it did, those who trusted in candidates, court appointments, and legislation to stem the tide of evil and ignite revival were left crushed and disillusioned.

BACK TO THE BASICS

Today, few of us see politics and legislation as the pathway to national revival. Instead, the political arena has become a mostly defensive battleground where we desperately seek to stem the tide of a growing legislative and judicial hostility toward biblical values.

We're no longer trying to impose our will on non-Christians. We're trying to keep non-Christians from imposing their will on us—and our churches.

If you haven't noticed, the culture wars are over.

We lost.

And while that fact might be a legitimate cause for disappointment, it's not a cause for despair. If our hope is firmly rooted in Jesus,

---

1   "Religion: Counting Souls," *Time*, October 4, 1976, http://content.time.com/time/magazine/article/0,9171,918414,00.html.

our salvation, and his certain return, we have far more to rejoice in than to be anguished about.

Jesus's promise to build his church is still in play.

So is his promise that the gates of hell can't hold us back.

But we'll have to change our game plan. We'll have to go back to the basics. The methods of the flesh and the methods of this world will have to be set aside, exchanged for the methods and weapons of the Spirit: prayer, obedient living, loving our enemies, and faithfully proclaiming the gospel.

These are the weapons that Daniel used. He brought great fame and glory to the Lord despite living his entire life under godless leadership, faced with a constant stream of military, political, and legislative setbacks. So did the early church in Acts. So can we.

Now having said all this, I want to make it perfectly clear that I am not saying politics are unimportant. And I am not saying Christians should stay out of politics. We live in a democracy. We have the right to influence the public debate. To neglect that right would be foolhardy.

I'm simply stating that it's a tragic miscalculation to place our hope in political solutions. At the end of the day, no matter how many elections we might win or how many laws we might pass, political power is fleeting. The tide always changes.

THE PROBLEM WITH MINISTRY ON STEROIDS

Politics is not the only bandwagon that fails to deliver. So does ministry on steroids: the big-budget, high-visibility programs and ministries that suck massive amounts of energy, resources, and money from the one thing God has ordained as his primary vehicle of evangelism and discipleship (more about that later).

Authentic movements of God tend to be organic. They're birthed by the Spirit and fueled by the Spirit. They're not dependent upon slick marketing campaigns, fancy flow charts, and fund-raising dinners.

That's not to say God can't use these things. He once spoke through a donkey. He collapsed the walls of a city with trumpet blasts. He fed five thousand from a lunchbox. He can do whatever he wants. But so far, grandiose plans and massive recruitment efforts have not been his method of choice when it comes to revival.

Authentic movements of God also tend to be unique. Even a casual study of Scripture shows that God seldom used the same method twice. Whether it was the great miracles and battles in the Old Testament, the healings of Jesus's day, or the miraculous expansion of the early church, there aren't many molds that he used a second time.

That's why a cottage industry of scholars who study past revivals in the hope of discovering and duplicating the recipe God used in the past strikes me as strange. The same goes for those who map out ambitious plans designed to mobilize the entire Christian community in the pursuit of a particular program or ministry.

That's not to say there is nothing to learn from studying how God worked in the past or that elaborate planning and prayer is a waste of time. It's simply to say that God seldom uses our game plan or follows our timetable.

I've learned not to put my trust in any ministry on steroids, no matter how many folks jump on the bandwagon. I've found that the results never match the hype. At the end of the day, the success or failure of God's kingdom doesn't depend upon our human efforts. All we can do is prepare the horse for battle. The results rest with the Lord.[1]

CASE IN POINT: *THE PASSION OF THE CHRIST*

But there is an even bigger problem than the disillusionment that our modern-day ministries on steroids tend to produce. It's the massive amounts of time, energy, focus, and money they suck away from the local church.

As a case in point, consider the excitement that surrounded the release of *The Passion of the Christ*, Mel Gibson's film depicting the final hours of Jesus's life. Many Christians were convinced it would ignite a spiritual tsunami. The organizers promised it would be a watershed event, shaking America out of its spiritual stupor.

Churches all across the country were recruited to get as many people as possible into the theaters to see it. Like many churches, we bought some tickets. We filled a theater. We watched a movie. And that was pretty much it.

It was hardly a watershed event. There was no discernible long-term impact. As far as I could tell, it did little to advance the kingdom. But it did do a lot to advance Mel Gibson's net worth.

That doesn't mean *The Passion of the Christ* was a bad thing. Indeed, some people came to Christ. Some made life-altering recommitments. But when all was said and done, it was just

---

1   Proverbs 21:31

another ministry blip on the radar screen. Here today. Gone tomorrow.[1]

And therein lies one of the biggest problems with our modern-day big-budget, high-visibility programs and ministries. They not only put our hope in something that can't deliver, but they also unintentionally sabotage God's primary ministry vehicle for evangelism and discipleship, the local church.

GOD'S PLAN A

Let's be honest. *Most* high-visibility ministries and programs operate independent of the local church. They may talk about their desire to be an extension of the local church. But in reality, they pretty much treat it as fertile ground for recruiting and fund-raising, not much else.

Admittedly, the local church is anything but sexy. It has a lot of problems. It often puts cherished traditions above its God-given mission. It's easily sidetracked. And it's done a lot of stuff that gives God a bad name.

But despite all that, the church in all of its local manifestations is the one thing Jesus said he would build and sustain. It's the pillar and foundation of truth, Satan's kryptonite, and God's plan A for making disciples.[2]

The fact is, anything that sabotages the local church sabotages the work of God, even if it's unintentional.

---

1   James 4:14; Ecclesiastes 1:11
2   1 Timothy 3:15. The Greek word for *church* literally means "assembly." It's a reference to the people gathered, not the building they gather in.

When it comes to raising a generation of Daniels (men and women with Daniel-like hope and courage), the only thing that will work in the long run is the same thing that has worked for the last two millennia: local churches.

Our seminaries, denominations, publishing houses, and media outlets are not up to the task. Neither are our parachurch ministries and the grandiose programs that flow out of them. But the church is different. Despite its flaws, whenever a group of Christians gathers together for prayer, worship, teaching, and accountability, Jesus promises to show up.[1] And when Jesus shows up, hope and courage are never far behind.

---

1   Matthew 18:20

HUMILITY: HOW CREDIBILITY IS EARNED

CHAPTER FOURTEEN
HUMILITY
The Forgotten Path

Daniel's hope gave him courage. But it was his remarkable humility that gave him favor in the eyes of his captors. In order to thrive in Babylon, he needed a strong dose of both.

Courage without humility leads to martyrdom.

Humility without courage leads to spinelessness.

But together, courage and humility can shake the very foundations of hell, advancing the kingdom of God into the most unlikely of places. Even in Babylon.

NOT JUST FORGOTTEN

Unfortunately, the path of humility is seldom trod today.

It's not that it's forgotten.

It's disdained.

No one wants to go there.

Especially men.

I don't think I've ever heard a dad say he wanted his son to grow up to be humble. It carries a weak and mostly negative connotation. When we speak of someone coming from humble stock, we don't mean it as a compliment. And when we talk about living in humble circumstances, it's not with envy.

Our modern-day definitions of humility tend to equate the word with low self-esteem, a soft and pliable disposition, lack of ambition, and a conscious effort to minimize or downplay all of our accomplishments.

No wonder most of us treat humility as a lofty ideal, something to strive for on occasion, though not something we want too much of.

But low self-esteem, a soft and pliable disposition, lack of ambition, and a denial of our strengths and accomplishments have nothing to do with biblical humility. They aren't the marks of spiritual maturity. They're the marks of insecurity.

The kind of humility Daniel had (and the kind that God calls us to have) is something altogether different.

BIBLICAL HUMILITY

To understand what biblical humility is, we need to clear out some of the most widely held but thoroughly unbiblical ideas and definitions that have made humility a path so few want to take.

It's Not Low Self-Esteem

Biblical humility is not synonymous with low self-esteem. The Bible actually commands us to have an accurate assessment of our strengths and weaknesses. We're not to think more highly of ourselves than we ought to think and we're not to think more poorly of ourselves than we ought. Instead, we're to gauge our gifts, abilities, strengths, and weaknesses with sound and sober judgment.[1]

Jesus was humble, but he also had a rather high opinion of himself. He claimed to be God. There's no way to equate that with low self-esteem.[2]

Daniel described himself and his friends as "young men without any physical defect, handsome, showing aptitude for every kind of learning, well informed, quick to understand, and qualified to serve in the king's palace." That sounds rather confident, even cocky to me. Those are hardly the words of someone with low self-esteem. Apparently, he liked what he saw in the mirror.[3]

There is no virtue in a lack of confidence or self-abasement. If we're handsome and well qualified to serve in the king's palace, Jesus expects us to know it, acknowledge it, and do something with it. We're not to be arrogant and look down on others. But there's nothing to be gained by trying to pretend that we're ugly with a marginal IQ.

It's Not a Lack of Ambition

In the same vein, humility doesn't negate ambition. Daniel and his friends were ambitious. They worked hard to graduate at the top of their class. Daniel sought to have his three friends, Shadrach,

---

1   Romans 12:3; Galatians 6:3–4
2   Matthew 11:29; John 10:30–33; 14:6
3   Daniel 1:4

Meshach, and Abednego, appointed as administrators over the prov-
ince. It's the first thing he asked Nebuchadnezzar to do after he was
placed in charge of all of Babylon's wise men.[1]

Or consider James and John. When they sent their mom to ask
Jesus to grant them prominent positions in his kingdom, he didn't
rebuke them for their ambition (or for their mama's-boy approach).
He rebuked them for their lack of understanding of what it would
take to get there.

If they wanted to be great, Jesus was fine with that. But he
wanted to make sure they understood the path to greatness was the
path of humble service, and the path to become first was the path of
serving like a slave.[2]

It's Not Downplaying Our Accomplishments

Finally, biblical humility doesn't mean we never tell anyone about
our successes or accomplishments or that we refuse to take joy in
them.

I remember talking to a friend whose dad was set on raising
humble children. He thought it was boastful to speak publicly of
their successes. So he never did. Even when someone else brought it
up, he quickly deflected the conversation to something else.

Sadly, the result was not humility. It was four sons with a "father
wound." To this day they grapple with a gnawing sense of insecurity.
They know their dad loved them. But they still aren't sure if he was
ever pleased with them.

---

1   Daniel 2:48–49
2   Matthew 20:20–28

Biblical humility is willing to be overlooked. It doesn't insist on public honor or acknowledgment. It doesn't trumpet status or accomplishments in an unseemly manner. But that's not the same thing as hiding or artificially downplaying our successes.

After all, the only reason we know all the great things Daniel did is because he wrote a book to tell us about them. Apparently God was good with it. He put it in the Bible.

It's Serving Others

At its core, biblical humility is simply serving others by putting their needs and interests above our own. It's treating others the same way we'd treat them if they were someone "important."

It doesn't mean we become a doormat.

It does mean we become a servant.[1]

Now I realize it's easy to talk about humbly serving others but not so easy to do in real life, especially when it comes to serving people we'd rather not serve. But that's what biblical humility does. It not only serves those who deserve it. It serves those who don't deserve it. That's why it's called *humility*.

When Abraham let his young nephew Lot pick whatever portion of the land he wanted, it was an act of biblical humility. As the patriarch of his family, Abraham had the right to the best land. But instead of selfishly keeping it for himself, he gave Lot first pick. And he was willing to live in whatever land was left over.

Ironically, Lot's selfish decision to take the best land for himself proved to be his undoing. It started him on a tragic path to destruction.

---

1   Philippians 2:3–5

Meanwhile, immediately after Abraham's generous act of humility and selflessness, God showed up and personally promised to give him everything he could see in all directions. Which is how biblical humility works. When we take the path of serving others, we end at the place where God's favor and blessing reside.[1]

But biblical humility doesn't stop with serving those who don't deserve to be served. It goes one step further. It even serves God's enemies.

When Jesus washed the feet of his disciples, he included Judas. And when he defined the kinds of neighbors we are supposed to love, he included everyone who crosses our path—friend, foe, and even religious heretics.[2]

DANIEL'S HUMILITY

That's the kind of humility Daniel had. He served his captors and wicked masters so well and loyally that he kept getting promoted. And with every promotion, his influence in Babylon grew greater, eventually leading both King Nebuchadnezzar and King Darius to proclaim Daniel's God as the only true God.[3]

Yet I'm afraid a modern-day Daniel would be harshly criticized. Many Christians would see him as a spiritual compromiser. He'd be accused of aiding and abetting the enemy.

---

1   Genesis 13:1–18; James 4:10
2   John 13:1–17
3   Daniel 4:34–37; 6:25–28

Today we are far more prone to isolate than to infiltrate. We keep our personal contact with godless leaders and institutions to a minimum. And when we do engage, it's more likely to be an adversarial confrontation than conducted in a civil conversation. It's no wonder our cultural influence is at an all-time low.

If we want to significantly influence our modern-day Babylon, we'll have to change our tactics. Instead of avoiding or attacking the godless leaders of our day, we'll need to begin to engage them in the same way Daniel did, humbly serving whomever God chooses to temporarily place into positions of authority.

It's the only way we'll ever earn the right to be heard.

Without contact, there can be no impact. Yet since the earliest days of the church, many well-meaning Christians have assumed that civil and friendly relationships with wicked and godless people are an implicit endorsement of their sin and values.

It's a problem the apostle Paul had to address in one of his letters to the Corinthians. They had misunderstood his instructions in an earlier letter when he'd instructed them not to associate with those who were sexually immoral, greedy, dishonest in their business dealings, or worshipping false gods.

They thought he meant to avoid non-Christians who lived that way. So he wrote again to clarify what he meant. He didn't want them to cut off from non-Christians who lived like hell. In that case, they'd have to leave the world. He wanted them to cut off from self-proclaimed Christians who lived that way.[1]

---

1   1 Corinthians 5:9–13

WITCH DOCTORS AND MISSIONARIES

It's always struck me as strange that a missionary who befriends the local witch doctor is praised for making relational inroads into the darkest parts of his mission field. He's a hero. We put a picture of him and the witch doctor on our refrigerator as a reminder to pray for him.

But if an American pastor befriends the local Imam, a Mormon bishop, a politician from the wrong side of the aisle, or a prominent leader in the gay rights or pro-choice movement, he'll be assailed for fraternizing with the enemy. His picture will be posted on blogs, and it won't be as a reminder to pray for him.

If we aren't careful, we can make the same mistake Jonah did. He not only hated the *sin* of the Ninevites; he hated the Ninevites. That's why he took off in the opposite direction when God told him to go to Nineveh to proclaim God's impending judgment. He feared that they would repent and God would spare them.

Sure enough, that's what happened. And when they repented and God relented his judgment, Jonah was one ticked-off prophet.[1]

When our passion for God overrides our compassion for lost people, something has gone terribly wrong. When we come to the point where we'd rather see judgment than salvation, we are no longer aligned with the heart of God. We've become more like Jonah than Daniel.

---

1   Jonah 3:1–4:11

CHAPTER FIFTEEN

RESPECT

Breaking Down Walls

Sarah was smart and articulate. She was also an open book. You never had to guess where you stood with her. If she thought something was wrong, unfair, or simply stupid, she'd let you know. She kowtowed to nobody.

A few months after she started coming to our church, she sat in my office explaining to me how she viewed the world. She thought most people were spineless, too easily pushed around. They lacked guts and boundaries. They had no idea how to stand up for the truth—or themselves.

She was also convinced that most people worried too much about what other people thought. She was proud to be different. She didn't care. If someone didn't like hearing the hard truth, that was their problem, not hers. And if someone didn't like the boundaries she'd set, that too was their problem, not hers.

She then went on to complain about a long series of unfair workplace environments, the clueless bosses she'd worked for, the disloyalty of former friends, and an idiot ex-husband.

Suddenly, in the midst of her diatribe, she stopped. She stared at the ground for a long time saying nothing. Then she began to tremble before collapsing on the floor in a flood of uncontrollable tears.

I sat there dumbfounded.

I hadn't seen it coming.

She didn't seem like the type.

Through her heaving sobs she asked me why God was so mad at her, why she couldn't keep a job, why her friends kept turning on her, and why she was so lonely.

I didn't have the heart to tell her.

Everything about her was a relationship repellent.

She thought she was honoring God by standing up for truth and justice. She thought she was protecting herself with strong boundaries. She thought refusing to "kiss up" to those in power was a sign of strength.

But Sarah's big problem was that she saw respect as a one-way street. She demanded it from others, but she gave it sparingly. They had to earn it.

Her approach to life and others was the antithesis of biblical humility.

Biblical humility offers respect to everyone. And it goes much deeper than the hollow "yes, sir" or "no, sir" of a Southern gentleman. It's the real deal, a heartfelt deference that comes from the recognition that *everyone* bears the image of God, no matter how marred that image might be.[1]

DANIEL-LIKE RESPECT

This is the kind of respect that Daniel and his three friends showed toward everyone they came across. They never copped an attitude. From their jailers to a series of wicked kings, they treated them all with a profound and humble respect. It didn't matter if they were seeking to be exempted from a nonkosher menu or firmly refusing to bow down to worship an idol.[2]

I find that their respectful attitude, words, and behavior were radically different from the anger and resentment that is so common among many of us today, especially when it comes to how we respond to those who are strongly opposed to our values and faith.

Genuinely Concerned for Their Best Interests

Daniel genuinely desired the best for his captors. Much like Joseph, he endeared himself to them with humble service and a heartfelt concern for their best interests.[3]

Consider the way he responded when God revealed to him that he was going to bring down the hammer on Nebuchadnezzar. Daniel told the king, "My lord, if only the dream applied to your enemies and its meaning to your adversaries!"[4]

---

1   Genesis 1:26–27; 9:6; James 3:9
2   Daniel 1:8–16; 3:16–18
3   Joseph's story is found in Genesis 37–50.
4   Daniel 4:19

I'm afraid I might have said something quite different. Something like, "I've got news for you, big boy. Your sins have found you out. God is about to judge you big-time—and it's not a moment too soon."

Willing to Accept God's Sovereign Assignment

Daniel's humble respect was tied to his firm belief that God is in control of who is in control. It wasn't merely a theological axiom. It was a reality he lived by.

He saw Nebuchadnezzar as God's servant, a wicked king allowed to reign for a period of time in order to fulfill God's sovereign purpose—in this case, the discipline and judgment of Jerusalem for the sins of its people.

Daniel wasn't respectful because Nebuchadnezzar deserved it.

He was respectful because God commanded it.

Unfortunately, Daniel's outlook and actions are incredibly rare today.

NOTHING HAS CHANGED

I've heard every possible excuse as to why Daniel's and Joseph's responses to godless masters and leaders won't work today.

None of them hold water.

No matter how bad things get, the path of humble service and respect toward those God has placed in temporary authority has always been the path God calls us to take.

Consider the words of Jeremiah, a contemporary of Daniel. He told the Israelites who were reluctant to serve the king of Babylon that they were wrong. God wanted them to humbly submit during his short season of power and authority.

> Do not listen to your prophets, your diviners, your interpreters of dreams, your mediums or your sorcerers who tell you, "You will not serve the king of Babylon." They prophesy lies to you that will only serve to remove you far from your lands; I will banish you and you will perish. But if any nation will bow its neck under the yoke of the king of Babylon and serve him, I will let that nation remain in its own land to till it and to live there, declares the LORD.[1]

The apostle Peter said much the same thing to those who were suffering under the thumb of the Roman government—and a crazy tyrant named Nero.

> Submit yourselves for the Lord's sake to every human authority: whether to the emperor, as the supreme authority, or to governors, who are sent by him to punish those who do wrong and to commend those who do right. For it is God's will that by doing good you should silence the ignorant talk of foolish people. Live as free people, but do not use your freedom as a cover-up for evil; live

---

1   Jeremiah 27:9–11

as God's slaves. Show proper respect to everyone, love the family of believers, fear God, honor the emperor.[1]

And here's how the apostle Paul put it:

Let everyone be subject to the governing authorities, for there is no authority except that which God has established. The authorities that exist have been established by God.[2]

The clarity of these commands is unmistakable. There's no way to get around it. Which is why I'm befuddled by many of the things I've heard on Christian radio, read in blogs, seen posted on social media, and heard in hallway conversations. There's a marked absence of Daniel-like honor and respect toward godless leaders and a great deal of ridicule, contempt, bitterness, and even hatred.

It's no wonder we keep losing influence.

We're building up walls instead of breaking them down.

The fact is, if we're unwilling to treat godless leaders with respect, we'll have no chance of influencing their decisions and actions. No one listens to people who look down on them with contempt or disdain. When we know that others don't like or respect us, we shut them out, become defensive, or go on the attack. Which is precisely how our culture has responded to Christians at large.

---

1   1 Peter 2:13–17
2   Romans 13:1

IT'S A LONG ROAD

It's important to realize that the path of humility doesn't always pay off immediately. In fact, it seldom pays off immediately—or even quickly.

Daniel did the right thing despite being kidnapped, castrated, forced to study the occult, having his name changed to honor a demon, and then thrust into the service of a wicked king. I'm pretty sure he had no idea how things would turn out. If you had told him, he wouldn't have believed you.

He didn't humbly serve his Babylonian captors because he expected a quick reward. He did it because it was the right thing to do.

The same goes for Joseph. He walked the path of humble respect and service, even though it seemed like every time he did the right thing, it brought the wrong results. He had to be the most shocked person in the world when in one fell swoop he went from a forgotten prisoner to second in all of Egypt.

It was only after the fact that he could look back and see that God was at work turning the things others meant for evil into good. Until that moment, he had no idea his greatest tragedy would become his greatest blessing.[1]

It's the same for us today.

The path of humble respect and service seldom pays off immediately.

It's not something we do for short-term gain.

It's something we do because God says to do it—whether it works out or not.

---

1   Genesis 50:19–20

CHAPTER SIXTEEN

PERSUASION

The Problem with a Spiritual Warfare Model

My friend Aaron tends to see everything through the lens of spiritual warfare. He's a self-appointed watchman and warrior for God. He envisions himself and his church as frontline soldiers in a great spiritual battle between the forces of evil and those who uphold biblical values.

As a result, most of his interactions with non-Christians are adversarial.

He does a lot of debating but very little persuading.

He's fallen into a common trap. He's replaced the paradigm of persuasion with the paradigm of warfare. His focus has subtly shifted from persuading the lost to fighting the spread of sin on all fronts.

When we shift from persuasion to warfare, we stiffen resistance to the gospel. Non-Christians don't want to live like Christians. When they feel pressured to do so, they fight back. And when people are fighting, there's one thing they never do.

Listen.

Once the battle has been engaged, no one listens.

SEEKING TO PERSUADE

Daniel and his friends never treated their captors as enemies. They
followed the advice of Jesus long before it was given. They loved their
enemies and did good to them.[1]

We're supposed to do the same thing. Our great assignment
is to go out into all the world and recruit Jesus followers, teaching
them to obey everything he taught us. Jesus never told us to create a
Christian nation, impose our standards on nonbelievers, or preserve
a particular culture.

He told us to win over the lost.

Those who trade the persuasion paradigm for a warfare paradigm often forget the awful cesspool that the New Testament church
was birthed in. The Roman Empire knew nothing of political free-
doms. There were no family values. Sexual perversion was the norm.
Life was cheap. Justice was out of reach for all except the rich and
powerful.

And even though Rome tolerated most foreign religions, it didn't
tolerate Christians. The early church suffered fierce persecution. All
but one of the apostles died a martyr's death.

Yet the focus of the New Testament is entirely upon changing
hearts, not changing governments or culture. When the biblical

---

1   Luke 6:27–36

authors speak of spiritual warfare, it's always framed in the context of our personal spirituality.[1]

WHO'S OUR ENEMY?

The warfare model focuses on the wrong enemy. Non-Christians are not the enemy. They're *victims* of the Enemy. Victims need to be rescued, not wiped out.

The apostle Paul spelled out the response we're supposed to have toward those who live like hell and actively advance the cause of the Enemy. It's not what many would expect.

> And the Lord's servant must not be quarrelsome but must be kind to everyone, able to teach, not resentful. Opponents must be gently instructed, *in the hope that God will grant them repentance leading them to a knowledge of the truth, and that they will come to their senses and escape from the trap of the devil, who has taken them captive to do his will.*[2]

Notice that these are people who are doing the will of the Devil. They're not just in his parade. They're leading the parade.

Yet the goal of our interactions is not to see God pour out his judgment upon them. It's to see him pour out his grace and mercy,

---

1   You can find more on this subject in my book *Mission Creep: The Five Subtle Shifts That Sabotage Evangelism and Discipleship* (Owl's Nest, 2014). The insights from 2 Timothy 2:24–26 are found in chapter 6.

2   2 Timothy 2:24–26

granting them repentance and knowledge of the truth. In other words, our primary goal is persuasion.

Notice also the attitude and specific actions we're called to take.

We're not to argue or quarrel.

We must be kind to *everyone*. And, yes, everyone means everyone. No exceptions. I checked the Greek. I was hoping it was a rare word for *almost everyone*. No such luck.

We must also be prepared to teach and explain the truth, but it must be done gently, without resentment. The apostle Peter put it this way: "Always be prepared to give an answer to everyone who asks you to give the reason for the hope that you have. But do this with gentleness and respect."[1]

Frankly, it's here that many of us can miss the boat. The more Babylon-like our culture becomes, the more our resentment builds, resulting in bitterness, slander, rumormongering, and harsh critiques that no one would characterize as a kind and gentle rebuke.

Many excuse their words by pointing to Jesus's harsh rebukes of the Pharisees and other religious leaders of his day. But they miss the point. Jesus didn't rail on the sinners of his day. He pursued them. It was the religious hypocrites who were attempting to keep the sinners at bay that he blasted.

Nebuchadnezzar was as evil as they come. He served a demonic god. He trashed Jerusalem and God's temple. He mocked God. He was unreasonable, hotheaded, vain, murderous, and cruel.

Yet every interaction Daniel had with him was respectful and gracious. He understood that every time we treat God's enemies as

---

1   1 Peter 3:15

our enemies, we harden their hearts and build up a wall that makes repentance all the more unlikely.

WHEN BABYLON PROSPERS, WE PROSPER

A final problem with the spiritual warfare paradigm is that it creates a false impression that success of the wicked means failure of the righteous.

It's one reason so many of us have a hard time humbly serving a profane boss or submitting to godless governing authorities. We assume that if they succeed, we fail. Yet that's not how it works.

Now obviously our submission to those in authority doesn't include sin. When offered a nonkosher diet, Daniel refused to eat it. His three friends chose a fiery furnace rather than bowing down to a golden statue of Nebuchadnezzar. And Daniel continued to publicly pray even after it was declared a capital offense.

But the fact remains, that when our leaders prosper, we prosper. And when our nation prospers, we prosper, even if it becomes as wicked as Babylon. Consider the words of Jeremiah to the Jewish exiles in Babylon.

> This is what the LORD Almighty, the God of Israel, says to all those I carried into exile from Jerusalem to Babylon: "Build houses and settle down; plant gardens and eat what they produce. Marry and have sons and daughters; find wives for your sons and give your daughters in marriage, so that they too may have sons and daughters. Increase in number

there; do not decrease. Also, seek the peace and prosperity of the city to which I have carried you into exile. Pray to the LORD for it, because if it prospers, you too will prosper."[1]

It's a principle that still applies. In order to bring fame and honor to the name of Jesus, we must bloom where we're planted. We're not here by accident. God has not only numbered our days, but he's also preordained when and where we spend them.

Daniel was assigned to Babylon. Joseph was placed in Egypt. The early Christians were asked to serve God in Rome. And we've been assigned to this time and this place. Our task is unambiguous. We are to proclaim the gospel to lost people in the hope they will repent and bow the knee. Our goal is to win them over, not to wipe them out.

But we'll never be able to persuade anybody if our knee-jerk response to those held captive to do the Enemy's will remains one of anger, resentment, disrespect, and scorn. We can't toss verbal Molotov cocktails in the name of Jesus and claim we're loving our enemies.

No one will believe us.

And no one should.

---

1   Jeremiah 29:4–7

WISDOM: THE POWER OF PERSPECTIVE

CHAPTER SEVENTEEN

WISDOM

Some Things Aren't Worth Dying For

One of the telling marks of immaturity is a lack of perspective. Waiting is not an option. Compromise is a dirty word. Everything is equally important. There are no nuances. Everything is black and white. And the immediate consequences are the only consequences that matter.

I remember when my kids were young. If I gave them the option of a day at Disneyland or a day spent helping me clean out the garage, they'd choose Disneyland.

No surprise there.

But even if I changed the deal and offered them a free college education and the keys to a brand-new house after graduation in exchange for helping me clean out the garage, they'd still take Disneyland.

At that age they had no ability to see the big picture or to comprehend the long-range consequences of their decisions. No child does. It didn't bother me in the least. But if they're still thinking that way at thirty, forty, fifty years old, it will break my heart.

In the same way, it's no big deal when new believers lack spiritual perspective.

It's to be expected.

But when longtime Christians still lack the wisdom of perspective, something has gone terribly wrong. When they choose earthly treasures we can't keep over heavenly treasures we can't lose or judge God's goodness by today's problems instead of Good Friday's sacrifice or respond to sinners with knee-jerk repulsion rather than the pursuing heart of Jesus, they're stuck in spiritual immaturity. And it breaks God's heart.

THE POWER OF PERSPECTIVE

One of the things that set Daniel apart was his great wisdom and the perspective that came with it. He never chose earthly security over heavenly treasures. He never judged God's power and goodness by Babylon's temporary success. And he consistently responded to the sinners around him with the redemptive heart of God rather than the resentment and bitterness of Jonah.

Even as a young man forcibly carted off to Babylon, he saw things clearly. He grasped the big picture and responded to his trials in light of it. His refusal to give in to a "woe is me" mind-set reminds me of a diary entry reportedly made by Matthew Henry the night after he was robbed.

Let me be thankful, first, because he never robbed me before; second, because although he took my purse, he did not take my life; third, because although he took all I possessed, it was not much; and fourth, because it was I who was robbed, not I who robbed.[1]

THE BEGINNING OF WISDOM

Daniel's wisdom was rooted in the fear of the Lord. He knew that God was not to be messed with. Only a fool spits into the wind. Only a fool takes God's commands lightly.[2]

That's why Daniel and his friends always chose the path of obedience even if it seemed certain to cost them their lives. They feared God more than a fiery furnace, a lions' den, or anything else their captors could throw at them.

Yet at the same time, Daniel knew that not everything was worth dying for. He knew the difference between sin and the things he found personally offensive and distasteful. And he never confused the two. He picked his battles wisely.

It's here that many of us can miss the mark. We tend to confuse what we don't like with what God forbids. So we get worked up and go to battle over things that would have caused Daniel to shrug his shoulders.

---

1   There are various versions of this quote. This one can be found at "Quotes and Notes," *Wholesome Words*, www.wholesomewords.org/devotion1.html.

2   Proverbs 9:10

Call Me What You Want

For instance, as we've seen, when Nebuchadnezzar changed Daniel's name to Belteshazzar, he sloughed it off. His friends did the same. They didn't care what they were called as long as it wasn't late to dinner.

That doesn't mean they liked their new names. *Belteshazzar* means "Bel's prince." It had to grate on him every time he heard it. It would be like calling a modern-day believer named Christian, Mohammad.

Yet despite the offensive nature of his new name, Daniel realized there was no direct biblical command that we be known by a God-honoring name. So he let it slide. It wasn't a hill to die on.

Frankly, I think a modern-day Daniel would be criticized for passively accepting a demon-honoring name. Many would think he lacked courage. But it wasn't a lack of courage (Daniel had plenty of that). It was an abundance of wisdom. He knew what was and wasn't worth dying for.

Teach Me What You Want

Daniel showed the same calm sense of indifference when he was forced to study astrology and the occult for three years. If it had been an elective, he would have skipped the course. But he had no choice. It was the core curriculum.

While God forbids us to practice astrology or the occult, the Scriptures say nothing about what we can study. So rather than putting his foot down and refusing to participate (as he did with the king's table and a nonkosher diet), he took the course. And he didn't sit in the back rolling his eyes and subtly expressing his displeasure. He sat in the front, studied hard, and graduated at the top of his class.

Doing so gave him the platform and credibility he needed once he entered the king's service to debunk Nebuchadnezzar's trust in these things. It even gave him the opportunity to introduce the king to the God Most High.[1]

Daniel's response was very different from the typical pattern of resistance and withdrawal so many advocate today. When forced to participate in workplace training that advocates New Age paradigms or so-called diversity, many of us are encouraged to opt out as if *taking* the course is the same as *endorsing* the course. But it's not.

The same goes for our response to some of the godless content taught in our public schools and universities. When we boycott classes we don't like, we unintentionally forfeit our right to speak to the issues raised. But when we follow Daniel's lead and work hard, graduating at the top of the class, people have to listen. We've earned the right to be heard.

Do What You Please

Daniel also had the wisdom to understand that godless people live godless lives. He never forced his righteous lifestyle on others. Even as he rose to positions of power, he didn't try to impose his walk with God on those who didn't know God.

It's a lesson many of us are slow to learn. I know. I flunked the test the first time I took it.

As a college and graduate student I worked night crew at a grocery store. It was an eye-opening experience. I thought I'd heard it all in the locker room. But the crass language and sexually charged

---

1   Daniel 2:46–49

conversations that took place each night in the aisles were far more deviant than anything I'd ever experienced before.

As a new Christian, I made the mistake of trying to shut it down. I told some of my coworkers that I was offended when they used the name of Jesus as a curse word. I let them know I was troubled by the constant degradation of women as sexual objects, and I despised the foul jokes and language that everyone else thought were funny.

I was sure God was pleased with me for taking a stand.

I was proud of my "godly influence."

But in reality, I had no godly influence. All I did was ostracize myself. Some of them cleaned up their act around me, but they mocked me behind my back. I became "preacher boy" and a few other names I won't put into print.

Taking a stand did nothing to draw them to Jesus. It simply confirmed their negative stereotype of Christians. They put me in their "Jesus freak" box and sealed the lid. We never had another serious conversation about life or Jesus again.

My problem was a lack of perspective. I thought their biggest issue was their garbage mouth and godless lifestyle. But their biggest issue was not knowing Jesus. By trying to enforce my Christian values and sensibilities upon them, I lost the chance to introduce them to the only One who could clean up their act and forgive their sins.

TOLERANCE

Finally, Daniel's wisdom also made him a man of great forbearance. He put up with an astonishing amount of evil and decadence. He was amazingly tolerant in the biblical sense of the word.

Rightly understood, tolerance is a trait we should all excel in. If tolerance means granting people the right to be wrong, we of all people ought to be known for our tolerance.

Unfortunately, that's not what tolerance means today. The word has been redefined. It no longer means granting others the right to be wrong. It now means that nobody is wrong. Those who dare to claim that some behaviors are actually morally wrong are written off as intolerant bigots. And ironically, they become the one group nobody is tolerant of.

While many of us bemoan the intolerance directed toward Bible-believing Christians today, we have no one to blame but ourselves. We're getting what we gave.

Back when Christianity was the dominant cultural religion, we often used our power to shut down those who advocated opposing agendas. We'd raise a fuss and force a college to disinvite a commencement speaker who advocated a godless agenda. We'd pressure sponsors to stop advertising on television shows we didn't like. We'd boycott non-Christian companies for making non-Christian decisions.

Now we're on the receiving end. As I write this, a TV show has recently been canceled because of the evangelical leanings of the host. A pastor has been disinvited from praying at the presidential inauguration because he had the audacity to teach what the Bible says about sexuality. And a national chain is under fire because the owners have donated to ballot measures considered antigay.

I often wonder what would have happened if we'd had the wisdom of Daniel when we were in control. What if we'd been tolerant in the biblical sense of the word? What if, rather than trying to silence those we strongly disagreed with, we'd let them have their say, secure in the knowledge that truth has nothing to fear?

My bet is we'd still be out of favor. But we'd have a far more level playing field from which to speak to the sins and issues of our day.

It's a mistake Daniel never made. Whether he was at the bottom of the food chain or near the top, he never tried to force his righteousness on others. He let pagans live like pagans, while living his own godly life in full view. Which is why when the time came for him to step forward and speak up, he'd already earned the right to be heard.

The wisdom to pick his battles prudently was one of the most important keys to Daniel's success and eventual influence in Babylon. While he was resolute in his refusal to sin, he was just as resolute in his commitment to overlook those things that were merely uncomfortable, offensive, or demeaning.

He knew there was a big difference between what he didn't like and what God forbade. He drew his lines in the sand where God drew the lines.

CHAPTER EIGHTEEN

SCAREDY-CAT CHRISTIANITY

When Fear Takes Over

I have a spear in my office.

It's not just any spear.

It's a witch doctor's spear—from a real-life demon-worshipping witch doctor.

I picked it up years ago on a trip deep in the Amazon jungle. I was there to visit two missionaries who were working with a small tribe that had only recently come into contact with the outside world.

I was only there for one night. But it was one of the most surreal experiences of my life. A few hours after sunset, the tribal chief and witch doctor went into his hut, snorted his homemade hallucinatory drugs, and began to alternately chant and scream at the top of his lungs for hours.

For one of only two times in my life, I knew for certain that I was in the presence of demonic power. His chants and screams were blood-curdling. Then suddenly they came to a halt. The abrupt ending and total silence that followed made it all the more eerie.

The next morning I approached him and asked through our translator if I could trade him something for the ceremonial spear he used during his incantations. He agreed. I can't remember what I gave him. But I came home the proud owner of a demonic witch doctor's sacred spear.

I hung it on my office wall. I thought it was cool. But from the reaction of some of my friends, you'd have thought I'd brought a demon home.

They were aghast. They couldn't believe I'd intentionally acquire something so "evil," much less hang it in my office. They were convinced that I was giving Satan a foothold. They predicted all sorts of horrible things would happen as a result. They feared it would endanger my family, contaminate my office, and put our church at risk.

They seemed to think that satanic power and influence could be spread like cooties on an elementary school playground.

When I protested that it was just a stick, they were unconvinced.

When I explained that I'd brought it home and put it on the wall as a personal reminder that he who is in me is greater than he who is in the world, they said I was naïve and questioned my theology.[1]

But I wasn't the naïve one. My friends were. They gave Satan way too much credit. They thought his evil spread by osmosis. They were what I call *scaredy-cat Christians.*

---

1   1 Corinthians 10:13; 1 John 4:4

SCAREDY-CAT CHRISTIANITY

Scaredy-cat Christians forget that Satan is a liar, the father of lies, and deception is his native tongue. They believe his boasts.[1]

He can boast all he wants. The fact is, he can't touch us without the Lord's permission. He's only powerful when we believe his lies. He has no power otherwise.

He doesn't gain a foothold when we participate in, hang around, or touch something that was once his. He gains a foothold when we sin. Evil is not some sort of contagious disease. It's a conscious choice. We don't have to worry about being accidentally contaminated.

Scaredy-cat Christians make two mistakes that Daniel never made. They add extra rules to Scripture, and they run away from anything they perceive to be spiritually contaminated.

Unfortunately, both of these behaviors sabotage our ability to infiltrate and influence the world we live in. They make a Daniel-like impact impossible.

LEGALISM

Legalism is simply adding extra rules to the Bible. It flows out of the best intentions. It seeks to promote righteousness. But it's far more likely to produce pride, isolation, and a reputation among non-Christians that we're weird—or at best quirky.

The typical non-Christian looks at legalistic believers a lot like tourists look at an Amish community. They're impressed with the

---

1   John 8:44

high level of commitment, enjoy the food, and like the furniture. But they think they're odd. They have no desire to become one of them.

If you haven't noticed, extrabiblical and legalistic rules are always *based* on the Bible. They're just not *found* in the Bible. That's what makes it so hard to win an argument with legalists. They have a verse for everything, even when the verses they quote have nothing to do with the rules they make.

Consider the legalistic rules that were added to the Sabbath. The law of Moses required that Israelites abstain from work. But the rabbis and religious leaders weren't satisfied to leave it with that. They had to help God out with a precise definition of what constituted work.

So they created a detailed rule book. They determined it was okay to pull your animal out of a ditch on the Sabbath, but you couldn't administer medical aid to your friend. They decided that was too much like practicing medicine, which was work.

That's the reason they were so angry with Jesus for healing on the Sabbath. They wanted him to wait until the next day. Their passion for their rules had drowned out their compassion for people, which always happens once legalism gets a foothold.

I remember as a new Christian being exposed to the same kind of extra rules. I was told that I shouldn't watch television because the Bible says to redeem the time and use it wisely. I was forbidden to have a beer because the Bible says don't get drunk. I couldn't dance because the Bible says to flee sexual immorality.

And I was told to eat right and get a lot of aerobic exercise because my body is the temple of the Holy Spirit.[1]

All of these were presented as biblical rules, though none were actually found in the Bible. And none of the people who forced them on me seemed to notice that Jesus ripped on these kinds of extrabiblical, man-made rules.[2]

The apostle Paul was just as harsh in his criticism of extrabiblical rules. In his letter to the Colossians, he said they were completely worthless, incapable of producing righteousness or restraining fleshly desires. Here's how he put it:

> Since you died with Christ to the elemental spiritual forces of this world, why, as though you still belonged to the world, do you submit to its rules: "Do not handle! Do not taste! Do not touch!"? These rules, which have to do with things that are all destined to perish with use, are based on merely human commands and teachings. Such regulations indeed have an appearance of wisdom, with their self-imposed worship, their false humility and their harsh treatment of the body, but they lack any value in restraining sensual indulgence.[3]

---

1   These rules were based on Ephesians 5:15–18 and 1 Corinthians 6:18–20.
2   Matthew 15:2–9; Mark 7:13
3   Colossians 2:20–23

The fact is, God doesn't need our help or want our extra rules. He got it right the first time. He's not up in heaven agonizing over a few things he left out of the Bible. He doesn't need an editor and he doesn't appreciate it when we add to his words.[1]

THE FEAR OF CONTAMINATION

Another sign of scaredy-cat Christianity is the unwarranted and unbiblical fear of spiritual contamination. Instead of redeeming that which the Enemy has defiled, scaredy-cat Christians run from anything remotely connected to the Enemy.

That's not to say we should take our Enemy lightly. Only a fool does that. But it is to say there is no need to panic every time he roars or run from everything he's ever touched. We're called to resist the Devil, not run from him. And when we do, he's the one who flees.[2]

That's why Daniel had no problem studying the language and literature of the Babylonians. He didn't care that it had pagan roots. He wasn't afraid to be in the presence of evil. He knew the power of his God.

Because he was a prominent wise man, it's inconceivable that Daniel failed to show up at special events set aside to honor Bel and the other false gods of Babylon. His role in the royal court would have made his participation mandatory. Yet he seemed to treat it as no big deal.

---

1   Proverbs 30:5–6
2   Jude 9–10; James 4:7

Scaredy-cat Christians see the world quite differently. They're afraid they'll be contaminated if they participate in anything that has pagan roots or a godless connection.

Consider the annual uproar over Halloween. A friend of mine throws a block party every October 31. He sees it as a great way to connect with his non-Christian neighbors. They seem to agree.

But he's often chastised by his Christian friends. They think he should pull down the shades and turn out the lights. They're convinced he's worshipping Satan. He and his friends think they're having a barbecue.

His Christian critics point to Halloween's pagan roots (though they seem to miss the fact that some scholars trace Halloween's roots to ancient Christian traditions). They believe that jack-o'-lanterns and trick-or-treating are remnants of a nefarious past. They note that Satan worshippers have claimed it as their high holy day.

They're genuinely fearful for his (and his children's) spiritual condition. They think evil is a communicable disease. They fear rubbing shoulders with a few wannabe Satan worshippers is enough to undercut everything Jesus did on the cross.

They also tend to apply this same guilt by association and past heritage to everything from stretching exercises to children's books. They always have a subliminal danger to warn us about. Yet if they were to apply this same guilt by association or past heritage consistently, they'd have to get rid of a lot of things they cherish.

They'd have to burn their King James Bibles.

The old king was hardly a paragon of virtue.

They'd also have to stop celebrating Christmas because the date we celebrate Christmas on has nothing to do with the Bible or early church tradition. It's tied to the winter solstice. In fact, the Puritans were so concerned about the pagan roots and traditions surrounding Christmas that they forbade any celebration of the holiday.

They'd also need to remove the pipe organ from any church that still has one. It too has questionable roots. It was originally considered the instrument of the Devil due to its use in profane and godless theaters. In fact, Martin Luther was assailed for bringing it into the church. But he decided the Devil shouldn't have all the good music.

Scaredy-cat Christianity makes no sense.

It fails to honor the glory of our God.

It forgets that greater is he who is in us than he who is in the world.[1]

---

1   1 John 4:4

CHAPTER NINETEEN

COMPROMISE ISN'T A DIRTY WORD

Mercy Trumps Sacrifice

Compromise isn't a dirty word.

It can be.

But it isn't always.

Unfortunately, for many of us, compromise carries a negative connotation. We see it as something the weak and the disobedient do. But in reality, it's something the wise do as well. They know what battles they can win and what battles need to be fought later.

Daniel obviously had to make some tough calls in regard to what he participated in and what he avoided. If we could go back and be flies on the wall, I'm not sure we would agree with every decision he made. We might even see some as inappropriate compromises. But the important thing is that God was good with them. He knew Daniel's heart, so he blessed his decisions, even if some were a bit sketchy.

This is something that fear-based Christianity misses. It tends to see God as an angry god looking for reasons to nail us. It forgets that Jesus was nailed to the cross for our benefit. He's not looking for reasons to punish us. He's looking for reasons to bless us. He values mercy over sacrifice.[1]

When it comes to navigating the tough calls of life, fear-based faith is terrified of making a mistake. That's why it has all those extra rules and boundaries. It's convinced that any accidental misstep or compromise will be dealt with harshly.

BLIND SPOTS

The fact is, we all have blind spots. And while the important commands of Scripture are crystal clear, there are plenty of things in Scripture that are far more nuanced and hard to understand.

Anyone who has ever changed his mind about a biblical or theological issue has by definition corrected a blind spot. And unless we want to claim we now know it all and will never again be corrected or shown anything new, we have to admit we still have some blind spots we're unaware of.

When we obey the light we have, God promises to give us more. The Bible describes the path of the righteous as being like the rising of the morning sun. At dawn it's hard to see much. At midday everything becomes clear.[2]

---

1   Hosea 6:6; Matthew 9:13
2   Proverbs 4:18

But in the meantime, sometimes all we can do is make our best guess and then trust God to understand our heart or to enlighten us if we're missing something.

Daniel didn't worry about what he didn't know. He worried about obeying what he knew. In situations where God spoke clearly, he did what God said. In those areas where it was less clear, he did what seemed best. He understood that there are some areas where God doesn't care what path we choose. He cares how we walk the path.

Meat Offered to Idols

For instance, in the early days of the church, there was no consensus about whether it was okay to eat meat that had been blessed by the pagan priests in a pagan temple. There were good arguments on both sides. Some said eating meat was tantamount to participating in demonic worship. Others said it was no big deal. After all, the idols in the temple were nothing more than man-made objects. They had no real power.

So they wrote to ask the apostle Paul who was right. He shocked them by saying both were right. God had not laid down a specific command. Each side needed to do what seemed best to them and to avoid judging those who chose a different path.[1]

Solomon's Blind Spot

There are also some times when we take the wrong path unintentionally. Our heart is right but our actions aren't.

---

1   Romans 14:1–15:7

That's what happened to Solomon. When he wanted to show his love and devotion to the Lord, he chose to do so at Gibeon with a massive sacrifice of a thousand burnt offerings. The only problem was that Gibeon was a high place (actually the most famous high place) and God had forbidden the Israelites to worship at high places.[1]

The high places in Israel had previously been dedicated to idol worship. When the Jews entered the Promised Land, they were supposed to tear them down. Yet for some reason they failed to do so. The people and the kings who followed continued to worship at them.

There's no way around it. Solomon was not supposed to be offering sacrifices to God at Gibeon. Yet it was there that God met him in a dream and promised to give him whatever he asked for.

When Solomon asked for wisdom to lead God's people, God was so pleased with his answer that he also gave him the things he didn't ask for: wealth, a long life, and victory over his enemies.

Why would God bless Solomon in the midst of his sacrifices at a forbidden high place? It must have been a blind spot instead of high-handed disobedience. And God chose to respond to Solomon's heart rather than his unintentional sin.

Frankly, that gives me great hope. Even when I don't get it right, God sees my heart.

COMPROMISE

In addition to understanding our blind spots, God also understands our weaknesses. He never asks us to do the impossible. He knows

---

1   Numbers 33:52

there are some situations so dicey that they call for compromise. There's no other viable solution. In a fallen world, sometimes we're forced to choose the lesser of two evils.

Two Midwives and a Prostitute

I think of God's command that we always tell the truth. Our yes is to be yes and our no is to be no. He's rather clear about it.

But when Pharaoh commanded the Hebrew midwives to kill every Hebrew boy at birth, they had no choice but to lie. They told Pharaoh that the Jewish women were so robust that they gave birth before the midwives could arrive.[1]

It was the same for Rahab the prostitute. She had no choice but to lie about hiding the Hebrew spies and the direction they departed. Otherwise they would have been killed. So she said, "They went *that* way," when they went *this* way.[2]

God rewarded the midwives with children of their own. He rewarded Rahab with a family and a place in the lineage of Jesus. Apparently he understood that sometimes we have to choose the lesser of two evils.[3]

A Guy Named Naaman

Then there's the strange story of Naaman, commander of the Aram army, one of Israel's enemies and tormentors.

---

1   Exodus 1:15–22
2   Joshua 2:1–21; James 1:25–26
3   Exodus 1:21; Matthew 1:5

He came down with leprosy and through a series of strange events found himself in the presence of the prophet Elisha. Then through a series of even stranger events he was healed. As a result, he became a believer in the God of Israel.

But when it was time to return home, he faced a dilemma. His master and king worshipped a false god named Rimmon. In his role as the commander of the king's army, Naaman had to enter the temple and bow down when the king did. So he made this request of Elisha:

> Your servant will never again make burnt offerings and sacrifices to any other god but the LORD. But may the LORD forgive your servant for this one thing: When my master enters the temple of Rimmon to bow down and he is leaning on my arm and I have to bow there also—when I bow down in the temple of Rimmon, may the LORD forgive your servant for this.[1]

Now you'd expect Elisha to say, "No way. You have to make a choice. You can't bow down in the presence of another god."

But that's not what he said. He told Naaman, "Go in peace."

In other words, he allowed him to enter and bow down in the temple of Rimmon when his master did so. He chose mercy over sacrifice.

That's what wisdom does. And that's what God wants.[2]

---

1   2 Kings 5:17–19
2   Hosea 6:6; Matthew 9:13

CHAPTER TWENTY

WHAT GOD WANTS
Why Faithful Is More Important Than Successful

I've always loved the eleventh chapter of Hebrews. It contains God's Hall of Fame. It's filled with the stories of faithful heroes. It starts out listing the famous greats like Noah, Abraham, Joseph, and Moses. But toward the end of the chapter, there's a sudden shift. Instead of continuing to list victorious heroes, the author turns his attention to those who didn't fare so well.

He speaks of faithful people who were rewarded with jeers and floggings, chains and imprisonment. He points to others who were stoned, sawed in two, or killed by the sword. He recalls those who spent the bulk of their life destitute, wandering in deserts, or living in caves.

Then he makes this shocking statement: *"These were all commended for their faith, yet none of them received what had been promised."* In other words, their spiritual victory didn't come in this lifetime. It was found in the next.[1]

There's always a danger in studying a victorious saint like Daniel because we can jump to the conclusion that if we do what he did, we'll get what he got.

But that may or may not be true.

As we saw earlier, all Scripture is given for reproof, correction, and instruction in righteousness. Daniel gives us a template for living in Babylon. But the book doesn't come with a promise that we'll have the same results.

We may emerge victorious like Abraham, Joseph, Moses, and Daniel. Or we may be persecuted, martyred, marginalized, and exiled like the unnamed but faithful saints listed at the end of Hebrews 11. The final outcome is up to God. It's out of our hands.

Our job is not to win the battle. It's to follow God's battle plan.

There will be times when following God's plan doesn't seem to be working. But to those who have Daniel-like wisdom that begins with the fear of the Lord, that doesn't matter. Even when God's way seems to lead nowhere, it's still the right path to take. He's always right, even when we think he's wrong. That's why we call him God.

I like the way the writer of Proverbs put it.

> Trust in the LORD with all your heart
>   and lean not on your own understanding;

---

1   Hebrews 11:35–39

in all your ways submit to him,

and he will make your paths straight.

Do not be wise in your own eyes.[1]

Winning or losing is not the right scorecard. Obedience is. When we do the right thing, we're being faithful. Even if we get the wrong results.

WHY INFLUENCE IS THE WRONG SCORECARD

Sometimes I hear preachers rip apart the American church because of our waning influence. Others implore us to get right with God because if we do he will pour out revival.

I wish it worked like that. But it doesn't.

Our cultural influence has far more to do with who is in political power than whether or not the church is living up to its calling. And the times of unique visitation that we call revivals have far more to do with God's sovereign grace than anything we do to produce it.

God draws straight lines with crooked sticks.

He always has.

It's foolish to give credit to the stick.

The Church in Rome

We often look to the New Testament church as the model of spiritual maturity and power. But it took a few hundred years for the early church to spread its influence to the point of significant cultural

---

1   Proverbs 3:5–7

impact. During most of those first three centuries it was a persecuted minority.

Don't miss that. We tend to think in terms of twenty to seventy years. But history is played out in centuries, not decades. What we call failure might well be the foundation of what God calls success. And what we call success might not be so great when we see it in the rearview mirror.

Powerful but Unfaithful

For instance, consider the final conquest of the Roman Empire by the early church. On the outside it looked like everything was great. The church's influence had finally reached a tipping point. Constantine decreed an end to the persecution of Christians and made Christianity the de facto religion of the empire.

At that point it looked like a great victory. But in hindsight, the ascent to political and cultural power was actually a great tragedy. It weakened the church. The more powerful it became, the more people joined in, not to follow Jesus, but to gain power and social acceptance. In other words, as the church grew more and more powerful, it became less and less faithful.

The Church in America

Much the same thing holds true in the history of the American church. The periods of our greatest influence were not necessarily the periods of our greatest faithfulness.

For instance, the glory days of *Father Knows Best*, family values, and stay-at-home moms weren't all they were cracked up to be. Certainly the laws, cultural norms, and media of that day were more aligned with biblical values than today. But once again, as in Roman days, a powerful church is not always a faithful church. It draws people for the wrong reason.

Frankly, if those days were really a spiritual Camelot, someone needs to explain to me how they produced a generation of sex-crazed, free-love, dope-smoking hippies who grew up to be self-absorbed boomers.

JESUS AND HIS APOSTLES

On the other hand, Jesus and his apostles had little cultural influence. Sure, Jesus drew huge crowds. But by the time he ascended into heaven, they had dwindled to 120 hiding out in an upper room.

As for the apostles, all of them except one died a martyr's death. That's hardly winning over the culture. Yet they were as faithful as they come.

Sometimes the culture responds to godly living and sometimes it doesn't. It's out of our hands. And that's where Daniel comes in. He shows us how to live in Babylon whether we're being promoted or imprisoned.

STANDING IN THE GAP

In the meantime, never underestimate the potential influence that just one Daniel-like Christian can have. You might think you're insignificant. But you aren't. Your role is far more important than you may realize.

Sodom and Gomorrah would have been spared if there had been just ten righteous people living there. Moses held back God's judgment on the Israelites when he stood in the breach pleading with God to spare them. One lone believer in a family can set apart the rest.[1]

Our God takes no pleasure in the death of the wicked. He'd much prefer they turn from their wicked ways and live. And as he told Ezekiel, he's always looking for someone to stand in the gap and forestall his judgment. There's no reason that can't be you or me.[2]

THE POWER OF ONE SMALL LIGHT

Finally, never underestimate the power of the light you reflect. You might think it's too dim to make a difference. It's not.

I learned this lesson years ago on a family vacation.

Let me tell you the story.

To begin with, I need to tell you that my wife is claustrophobic. Not crazy claustrophobic—but you can see it from there. So I assumed that when we visited the Carlsbad Caverns, she would wait above ground in the gift shop and information center while the rest of us went below to take the tour.

To my surprise, when the gigantic elevator arrived to take us down to the caves, she decided to join us. When the doors opened, the cavern was so large and spacious that her fears melted away. She even decided to go on the tour with the rest of us.

---

1   Genesis 18:20–33; Psalm 106:19–23; 1 Corinthians 7:14
2   Ezekiel 22:30–31; 33:11

As we waited in line to buy tickets, a group from a previous tour exited. One of them said, "I loved it when they turned out the lights!"

Oh no, I thought.

What do I do now?

Should I tell her?

Should I ignore it and create a family memory—then ask for forgiveness later?

As I pondered what to do, my moral dilemma was solved. Nancy had heard the remark. She turned to me and said, "Did he say they turn out the lights?"

"Yes," I replied, "but it's only for a few seconds."

"Are you sure?" she asked.

"Yes, I'm sure," I said. "Trust me, I'm a pastor."

So she did. Our entire family went on the tour. It was a great experience. Mostly. Right up until the end.

As the tour drew to a close, the guide told us to take a seat. He then began to explain the utter darkness that speleologists have to deal with. There's no trace of light, so there's nothing for their eyes to adjust to. It's pitch black. You can wave something in front of your eyes and you won't see a trace of it.

Then to prove his point, he reached down and unplugged the electrical cord that lit our pathway. Instantly we were plunged into total darkness. About five seconds later, I realized that his demonstration was going to last more than just "a few seconds."

As I sat there feeling guilty, wondering how to best apologize to my wife, I suddenly felt a sharp pain followed by the sensation of blood dripping down my arm.

I'd been bitten by a bat.

Then the bat spoke.

It said, "I will never trust you again!"

I instantly tried to recall the name of every marriage counselor I knew. I figured I'd need one. Maybe even some career counseling as well, especially since the words *divorce* and *pastor* don't fit together real well.

As Nancy hung on and squeezed my arm in panic, I remembered something. My oldest son was wearing a brand-new Timex Indiglo watch. It was one of the early models, so the light it produced was pathetic. If you pushed the button to see the time at night, you still had to get a flashlight to read what it said.

But at this point, his watch was my only hope. I told Nathan to push the button on his watch. He did. Instantly we could see the ground and our feet.

The bat let go.

My marriage was saved.

And I learned an important lesson.

Actually I learned two lessons. The first was to never trick my wife into participating in anything remotely claustrophobic. The second was that the darker it gets, the more powerful the tiniest of lights becomes.

My son's pitiful Indiglo watch shone brightly in the utter darkness of a cave. Yet a person could hardly tell it was on when pressing the button under the evening stars.

It's the same with us. The darker it gets, the brighter our tiny light shines.

Don't buy the lie that you don't matter. You do. Don't buy the lie that your response to the evil in your workplace, community, family, and our nation doesn't matter. It does.

We just have to push the right buttons. They're called *hope*, *humility*, and *wisdom*.

It's what Daniel did thousands of years ago.

It's what God asks us to do today.

It's how he thrived in his Babylon.

And it's how we can thrive in our own modern-day Babylon.

Additional Books by Larry Osborne

DISCIPLESHIP/SPIRITUAL FORMATION

ACCIDENTAL PHARISEES

Zealous faith can have a dangerous, dark side. While recent calls for radical Christians have challenged many to be more passionate about their faith, the downside can be a budding arrogance and self-righteousness that "accidentally" sneaks into our outlook. Christians stirred by calls to radical discipleship, but unsure how to respond, will be challenged and encouraged to develop a truly Christlike zeal for God.

10 DUMB THINGS SMART CHRISTIANS BELIEVE

People don't set out to build their faith upon myths and spiritual urban legends. But somehow such falsehoods keep showing up in the way that many Christians think about life and God. These goofy ideas and beliefs are assumed by millions to be rock solid truth… until life proves they're not. But it doesn't have to be so. In this delightfully personal and practical book, Larry Osborne confronts ten widely held beliefs that are both dumb and dangerous.

SPIRITUALITY FOR THE REST OF US

If you've ever wondered why all the books on spirituality and the inner life are written by introverts with big vocabularies; if you find that you or those around you don't fit the mold; if you've grown weary of one-size-fits-all formulas for spiritual growth—then this book is for you.

MISSION CREEP

When Jesus sent out a ragtag team from Galilee with the expectation that they would evangelize and disciple the world, they pulled it off as a natural and spontaneous outworking of their faith. Yet 2,000 years later, this same natural and spontaneous process has been turned into a complex and highly programmed skill left to the professionals. This book exposes what's gone wrong and the five subtle shifts that sabotage our best efforts to reach the lost and bring them to full maturity.

LEADERSHIP

INNOVATION'S DIRTY LITTLE SECRET

Most books on innovation make it sound as if successful innovation is the end result of a carefully followed recipe. But the simple fact is that when it comes to any new venture, failure is the surest horse to bet on. What sets apart the serial innovator from the one-hit wonder? In *Innovation's Dirty Little Secret*, Larry Osborne reveals the hidden secret behind serial innovation and shows leaders how to navigate the landmines of innovations in ways that will provide new levels of stability and creativity to any organization.

STICKY TEAMS

Serving as a church leader can be a tough assignment. Whatever your role, odds are you've known your share of the frustration, conflict, and disillusionment that comes with silly turf battles, conflicting vision, and marathon meetings. No doubt, you've asked yourself, "How did it get this way?" This book exposes the hidden roadblocks, structures, and goofy thinking that all too often sabotage the health and harmony of even the best intentioned ministry teams. It is filled with practical and seasoned advice on what it takes to get a leadership board, ministry team, and entire congregation headed in the same direction, sticking together, unified, and healthy for the long haul.

STICKY CHURCH

In *Sticky Church*, author and pastor Larry Osborne makes the case that closing the back door of your church is even more important than opening the front door wider. He offers a time-tested strategy for doing so: sermon-based small groups that dig deeper into the weekend message and tightly Velcro members to the ministry. It's a strategy that enabled Osborne's congregation to grow from a handful of people to one of the larger churches in the nation—without any marketing or special programming. *Sticky Church* is an ideal book for church leaders who want to start or retool their small group ministry—and Velcro their congregation to the Bible and each other.

*For information on bulk orders, please contact
Erica Brandt at Erica@northcoastchurch.com*